WITHDRAWN

Queen Victoria's
Children

The Princess Victoria (Queen Victoria) aged four years
by S. P. Deny

Queen Victoria's Children

DAPHNE BENNETT

ST. MARTIN'S PRESS
NEW YORK

Dedicated
by gracious permission
to
Her Majesty Queen Helen of Roumania
great-granddaughter of Queen Victoria
and granddaughter of Queen Victoria's eldest child

Contents

Illustrations

Foreword and Acknowledgements

THE ONLY EXCUSE for yet another book about Queen Victoria, her husband and her family is that the author has had access to new material which throws fresh light on their personalities. By the gracious permission of Her Majesty the Queen, to whom I express my deep sense of gratitude, new material was put at my disposal in the shape of private letters, journals and other papers in the Royal Archives at Windsor. These made clear beyond all doubt that Queen Victoria's children enjoyed a warmth of family life and an intimacy with their parents rare in a century when it was usual for the children of the upper classes to be left entirely to the tender mercies of nurses, governesses and tutors.

The key to this difference between Queen Victoria's family and the families of her subjects was her own and Albert's discovery that they really liked children and were fascinated by watching them grow and develop. Albert took the lead in this, as in so much else; 'a capital nurse', the Queen called him in the early years of their marriage, and later on he turned out to be a father who took the greatest pleasure in teaching the four eldest children himself. Three of them, at any rate, were intelligent by nature, but there can be no doubt that Albert considerably developed their natural talents.

Sadly, by the time the five youngest were of an age for the same guidance Albert was dead, and their lives were the poorer without him. In their various ways, they suffered severely from their mother's total collapse at the loss of a husband she worshipped and from her subsequent inability to restart her life. She could not even take any real interest in the younger children, who still needed a parent's care, since she felt that the future held nothing for her and longed with all her heart for life to return to what it had been before 14 December 1861. She was (as she said many times) like a lost child herself, not understanding where she was going or why she had to live on, and in her anguish she forgot what her husband had told her about their children's highly individual characters and the care, attention and training each would need before marriage claimed them.

My purpose in writing this book has been to show the varying characters of these nine brothers and sisters and the effect their personalities—different in themselves, and made more different by their father's premature death—had on a family where the eldest was seventeen years older than the youngest. They were not docile children (with such passionate and strong-minded parents that would have been impossible), but could on occasion be as outspoken, defiant, rude and rebellious as any others. But the firm foundations of affection and parental care gave them all a sense of security which enabled each to withstand the many vicissitudes of the different lives they were to lead.

I am grateful to Sir Robin Mackworth-Young, the Queen's Librarian, who has given me most valuable guidance now, as in the past. My warm thanks are also due to Miss Jane Langton of the Royal Archives, who unselfishly gave up much of her precious time to help me.

Paintings from the royal collection are reproduced by gracious permission of Her Majesty the Queen. The painting of Queen Victoria as a child is reproduced by permission of the governors of the Dulwich Picture Library.

Mrs Joanna Sanders has once more typed my manuscript impeccably; I offer her my grateful thanks.

Daphne Bennett
Cambridge
September 1979

Prelude

'Family life in all its unruffled harmony is a
source of unimagined joy'

QUEEN VICTORIA ALWAYS said that she had a sad childhood. Poor,
closely-guarded, deprived of companions of her own age—her
half-sister Feodora was many years older—she had to depend for
company on her large collection of dolls, many of them wearing
dresses stitched by the youthful princess herself. However, her life
could not have been quite as gloomy as she remembered, for she
was by nature a merry child and there are several contemporary
accounts of her 'silver laughter' ringing out inside the old walls of
Kensington Palace or of her singing to herself as she played in the
gardens under the eyes of her mother, Victoire, the widowed
duchess of Kent, or of her governess Fräulein Lehzen.

In recollection she was possibly thinking less of her lack of
friends—since children are able to conjure up satisfactory play-
mates out of their imagination—than of the atmosphere of quarrels
and jealousies inevitable in a household of women. As she grew
older the sense of strain caused by these quarrels harmed her extrovert nature and drove her into herself, so that she learned to confide
in no one. 'I had led a very unhappy life as a child', she wrote to
her eldest daughter in 1858 soon after the latter's marriage, 'I had
no scope for my very violent feelings of affection—no brothers or
sisters to live with—never had a father . . . I did not know what a
happy domestic life was.' Memories of this early wretchedness
were a powerful reason why, at least until 1861, she devoted so
much thought and care to the upbringing of her children.

Far more serious than the backbiting of the household were the
feuds carried on by the Prince Regent (later George IV) and then
by his successor William IV against Victoria's mother. The Prince

Regent loathed the House of Coburg to which Victoire of Kent belonged, most unfairly cursing the whole tribe for what he believed to be their share in bringing about his disastrous marriage to Princess Caroline of Brunswick. His fury extended to Prince Leopold of Saxe-Coburg who had the temerity to marry his only daughter, Princess Charlotte of Wales, heiress presumptive to the throne. In fact Leopold had been a thorn in his side during the whole of his short-lived happiness with Charlotte (she died after only two years); the newly-married couple were so popular— crowds cheered enthusiastically whenever they appeared in public —that the Regent could not help being put out. He vented his spleen on Victoire, enjoying malicious gossip about her (which he knew to be false) and allowing it to spread. When his brother the duke of Kent died at Sidmouth on 23 January 1820, after a brief illness, all the Regent did for the penniless widow and her eight-months-old daughter was to assign her (but grudgingly) a suite of rooms in Kensington Palace so long as she kept out of his way. Satisfied that he had done all that was required, he washed his hands of his sister-in-law and her child and had nothing more to do with them.

Without money or friends and with hardly a word of English to her name the duchess, who already had a teenage son and daughter by her first marriage to the Prince of Leiningen, would certainly have starved had not her brother Leopold made the little family an allowance of £3,000 a year (later raised to £5,000) out of the £50,000 annuity he still drew from the English exchequer as husband of the dead Charlotte. Even with this bounty the duchess's position was pitiful. At odds with the Palace, her husband's creditors at the door, she struggled alone without a single adviser to bring up her family in a foreign country.

It was in this lonely atmosphere that Victoria lived as a child, and at that time the odds against her coming to the throne were heavy.

Princess Charlotte had died giving birth to a still-born son in October 1817. She and her husband had already found such a warm place in the hearts of the English that there had been general satisfaction when it became known that she was to have a child, for this meant that none of her profligate uncles would ascend the throne. Charlotte's death shattered this hope and left the country desolate.

What was to happen now?

The prospect was bleak. The Prince Regent hated his wife and refused to live with her again; his only two married brothers were childless, while the others lived openly with mistresses. Something would have to be done to save the Hanoverian succession. Parliament bluntly told the royal dukes that if they wished to retain their allowances they would have to put away their mistresses and speedily take lawful wives young enough to bear children. All except one (the duke of Sussex) went to the altar with shameless haste. Edward duke of Kent discarded Julie St Laurent, who had been faithful to him for twenty-eight years and borne him ten lusty children, chose for his bride Victoire, the thirty-year-old daughter of the duke of Coburg and widow of the Prince of Leiningen, whom he had met for the first time the previous summer, and married her on 29 May 1818. A daughter, Victoria, was born to Edward and Victoire a year later on 24 May 1819. Although Edward's brother William had also married by this time, none of his children survived for long and thus within a space of eight years it was certain that after George IV and William IV had died, Victoria of Kent would become Queen of England.

Joyless though her life was in Kensington Palace, the duchess of Kent—a widow with a baby daughter within two years of marriage—followed her brother Leopold's advice not to return to Germany but to stay and bring Victoria up as an Englishwoman, in case she should succeed to the throne.

The duchess was young and strong, and having decided to stay and sit it out she planned to give Victoria the best education within her means. Many sacrifices would have to be made, but she set about her economies with cheerful good sense, resolving that whatever happened she would see to it that her child was equipped with all the accomplishments that befitted a queen. She had great faith in the governess whom she had brought with her from Amorbach to teach her elder daughter Feodora. This was Louise Lehzen, whom she now put in charge of the whole of Victoria's education, save that Latin and religious instruction were assigned to the Reverend George Davis, a liberal evangelical clergyman. Victoria had a flair for languages and often spoke German with Lehzen, but apart from this Lehzen's teaching was narrow and prejudiced, as the duchess of Kent discovered later. As for Mr Davis, Victoria soon found that she could twist him round her little finger, and shamelessly did so whenever she was bored. Part of Lehzen's teaching was done by reading aloud, often when Victoria was having her hair brushed, but the choice of book was frequently very dull and the child's attention often wandered. This was not entirely Lehzen's fault, since novels were strictly forbidden because the duchess thought them trash and did not want her daughter's mind contaminated. Victoria had never read a novel until her husband introduced her to the delights of fiction, and was at first taken aback to see how he revelled in them.

Although the duchess spent far more than she could afford on making Victoria an accomplished young woman, she did not make a very good job of it because she had no one reliable to guide her. Almost the only positive results of the education she gave her daughter seem to have been a good singing voice (which even Mendelssohn admired), a talent for sketching, a love of dancing which lasted into old age and—above all—the pure English accent which Victoria's good ear and her mother's insistence enabled her to acquire. At all events, Queen Victoria laboured in later years under a feeling of inferiority because of an inadequate education, and determined that her own children should never suffer in the same way.

Meanwhile Albert was growing up in Coburg. Born on 26 August 1819, he was three months younger than his first cousin Victoria. By a curious coincidence they were brought into the world by the same obstetrician—strangely enough for those days a woman—the well-known Mlle Siebold. There was another early parallel between them too. Victoria never knew her father, hence her continual search for a surrogate father-figure; Albert scarcely remembered his mother, although he always revered her memory and named one of his children after her.

Albert's father duke Ernst I of Saxe-Coburg had married Luise, the only child of duke Francis of Saxe-Gotha-Altenburg, when she was only sixteen and he already a man of the world. Despite the birth of two healthy sons, Ernest and Albert, the marriage was soon on the rocks, and when the boys were four and three their parents separated. Two years later they were divorced and the children never saw their mother again. If duke Ernst had not been a good husband, he was an even worse father. He alternately bullied and neglected his children, who feared him more than they loved him; nevertheless, after the fashion of the day, they always wrote and talked of him respectfully, even affectionately.

When they were growing up, Ernest and Albert lived in Coburg in Thuringia where their father ruled with almost absolute powers. Although duke Ernst had two palaces in the town of Coburg, the home the boys loved best (Albert passionately so) was the Rosenau, a little hunting lodge four miles away in the country. Here duke Ernst seldom came except for a boar-hunt, preferring the bright lights of continental cities which he visited for long periods at a time accompanied by one or other of his mistresses. Yet despite the feudal surroundings in which he was reared, Albert received an excellent education, one that was surprisingly modern and as well geared to science as to mathematics, Latin, history and literature, so that his mind was open and receptive to all the new ideas which were just then beginning to circulate. A very exceptional young man was chosen to guide Ernest and Albert through the hazards of this modern education: Herr Florschütz, a graduate of the university of Munich and learned beyond his years. He was picked out by Leopold (King of the Belgians since 1830) and his confidential adviser Baron Christian Friedrich Stockmar, who was later to have such a powerful influence on the lives of Victoria and Albert.

In the atmosphere of unruffled calm (so different from that created by his father) which surrounded everything Florschütz did, Albert's talents developed by leaps and bounds; his reading widened and his skill in some of his leisure interests (music, geology and painting, for instance) increased until it was almost up to professional standards. It had been impressed on Florschütz that one of his duties was to make Albert aware of the larger world outside Thuringia which, as a younger son, he would one day have to enter and where he would have to compete with others on equal terms. If Albert was lazy or showed signs of forgetting this, Florschütz would punish him quite sharply and say in English 'don't forget, the race is to the swiftest'. It became quite a joke between the boys.

Albert might have dreamed his life away, with his books, his piano, his dogs and his horses in the Rosenau ('the paradise of our childhood'), had not Leopold and Stockmar decided otherwise. For despite the bullying of his father (duke Ernst excused his cruelty as 'making men of the boys'), which often made Albert sick with misery and drove him to hide his feelings even more than Victoria, he enjoyed long periods of pure happiness when he knew his father was miles away and would not be home for months. Then he would dream of becoming a great philosopher, perhaps the first prince to be made a university professor. Ambitions of this kind would have horrified Stockmar and set his head spinning, had he known of them. But Albert liked the idea so much that he wrote long (and, it must be said, boring) essays, packed full of philosophical meanderings, showing how the world could be changed for the better. These essays gave him enormous satisfaction and he hoped one day to turn them into a book. He was still very young.

By temperament Albert was complex: shy, sensitive, affectionate and passionate, in youth much given to bouts of quick temper, ready to lash out at the slightest provocation with his fist or tongue. He liked his own way and would go to great lengths to get it, a characteristic his tutor deplored and endeavoured to correct. Yet Florschütz was perceptive and saw from the beginning that Albert might go far if properly handled. King Leopold too thought Albert an unusual boy, and because he was a man of large ideas he made up his mind that Albert should become consort of the Queen of England, a position that had so nearly been his. He laid his plans with meticulous care, arranging for Ernest and Albert to be invited to Kensington for Princess Victoria's seventeenth birthday ball. The visit was not altogether a success. Victoria thought Albert unsophisticated, Ernest overbearing, and when they parted they hardly cared if they saw each other again. Six months at Brussels followed to broaden the mind. Then came eighteen months at the university of Bonn, where Albert was blissfully happy attending lectures in mathematics and philosophy but also taking an active part in every kind of student life and winning popularity and prizes for his skill in fencing and skating. He was still at Bonn in 1837 when he heard that Victoria had become Queen, an occasion he marked by a polite letter of congratulations. Her reply did not please him; its tone seemed condescending and haughty, quite absurd from one cousin to another. But he had no time to brood on it for he was whisked off to Italy for six months, with Stockmar as guide and mentor, to gain the kind of polish Victoria had told her uncle that he lacked. Shortly before the Italian journey Leopold told Albert that he hoped that one day he and Victoria would marry, but by the time of his return Leopold had to break the news that the Queen had written to say she did not intend to marry anyone for at least three years. The insolent tone of the letter angered Albert, but now he knew exactly how to deal with such nonsense. Coolly he asked his uncle to give Victoria a message: if they liked each other when he next came to England, it must be marriage within a reasonable time or not at all; that was his final word.

In the early autumn of 1839 Albert and his brother came again to England, rather against Victoria's wishes. Leopold had pleaded just for 'a short holiday for your cousins', banking on Albert's good looks and assured air to win the day. He was not mistaken. Victoria found Albert wildly attractive, so much handsomer and more confident than she remembered. Albert, who was prepared for the worst, thought Victoria a vision of loveliness, not cross-grained and selfish as before, but kind and concerned. It was love at once on both sides. They were married three months later, on 10 February 1840, a day that Victoria always kept sacred to the end of her life.

By the beginning of May they knew they were to become parents. In order to calm Victoria's fears (childbirth was 'the only thing I dread'), Albert tried, with remarkable maturity for his twenty years, to awaken her interest in the child's upbringing, a subject which excited him very much. He met with more success than he dared hope; before long Victoria too began to show a lively concern in the plans he had mapped out for the education of her heir (for of course they assumed that the first would be a boy). On one thing they were determined: their children should enjoy their parents' company as much as affairs of state would allow, for they had been shocked to learn how much the children of George III had suffered from being left to their own devices. In this they never faltered; the children were brought up knowing their parents far better than was usual at that time and became accustomed to turn only to them for advice and guidance.

In 1840 neither of them knew the slightest thing about babies (Albert had not even held one in his arms) but they felt so confident about their own ideas that they wrote them down at once in the form of a joint memorandum. Albert of course was the leading spirit, and for that reason the fragments that survive resemble the long and boring essays which he wrote when a student at Bonn, showing how the world could be reformed, and were lofty in conception, idealistic and far removed from real life. The perfect child was to develop into the perfect prince, a superman, calm, wise and all-knowing:

The boy should be taught early that thrones and sound order have a stable foundation in the moral and intellectual faculties of man, that by addressing his public exertions to the cultivation ot these powers in his people and by taking their dictates as the constant guides of his own conduct, he will promote the solidity of his empire and the prosperity of his subjects.

There then followed a rigmarole on hours of work, exercise and relaxation which future historians were to read with the greatest seriousness, condemning its author as harsh, cruel and insensitive, quite forgetting that the whole memorandum was simply the work of a high-minded but inexperienced young man carried away by enthusiasm in the face of a new problem. Stockmar, who was given the document to read, knew differently; he returned it with the dry comment that if the regime were adhered to the child for whom it was intended would surely die of brain fever.

Even Stockmar was not free of such high-flown thoughts himself, but in his own contribution to the upbringing of the royal children he does make two simple yet sound observations: he warned Victoria and Albert never to make the mistake of educating their children abroad, quoting as his example three of the Queen's uncles who were given a continental education. Although they were no worse than their brothers who had been educated entirely in England, their faults were magnified tenfold in the public mind because they were 'foreign'. His second point was even more crucial, particularly as Victoria and Albert had never thought of it—they should appoint a lady of rank as head of the nursery who 'must be well-educated and of irreproachable character. They must give her their absolute trust and support, for without this confidence education lacks its very soul and vitality. They must place about the children only those who are good and pure, who will teach not only by precept but by living example, for children are close observers and prone to imitate those they see or hear—whether good or evil.' As the years wore on Victoria and Albert came to realise how true this last remark was, and they always remembered it when employing a new governess or tutor. In 1866 Victoria repeated Stockmar's words to her eldest daughter Vicky: 'children's faults often proceed from the people about them —the damage done by an injudicious person be he ever so well meaning is not to be told. . . .' The lesson had sunk in.

A measure of Victoria and Albert's inexperience and lack of confidence in nursery matters is shown by what Stockmar called the 'injudicious start' which they made despite the long and earnest thought they gave the matter. Their biggest blunder was to consult the Archbishop of Canterbury, for he knew nothing at all about governesses and nurses; however he did have a friend with a poor relation whom he wished to see employed. The consequence was the appointment of the ineffective Mrs Southey (cousin of the poet), who could manage neither the nurses nor the children. Within two years there had to be a clean sweep, and in 1842 she was replaced by the woman Stockmar had had in mind from the beginning—the former Sarah Spencer, widow of the third Lord Lyttelton, who had been Lady in Waiting to the Queen since 1838. She possessed intelligence, patience and humour in abundance combined with a passionate love of children. With such a person in charge Victoria's forlorn words to Lord Melbourne—'our occupation prevents us from managing these affairs as much our own selves as other parents'—no longer mattered. Under the new governess the nursery became a haven where both parents were welcome and where they found relaxation from affairs of state. 'To guide these precious children along the right path' was a task Lady Lyttelton took seriously but with a sense of pleasure and fulfilment, glad that in old age (she was just over fifty!) she could still be of use. Her remarks to the Queen on the children's progress are a mine of information on their different characters, detailed and honest to a fault although never unkind, for she came to love them all dearly and always cared for their welfare even after she had left royal service. For the eight years during which Lady Lyttelton lived in close proximity with them, we get through her eyes a clear insight into the life of the royal parents and their children. She reveals something very different from the generally accepted picture of sternness and formality which surprisingly still survives.

Because she was conscientious to a fault, Lady Lyttelton every night wrote a detailed report on her charges, their diet, general health and mental progress and sent it early next morning to the Queen, who always read it at once. Facts about the children's health take up the largest part. Vicky had gripe too often, Bertie a continual running nose, while Alice never cut a tooth without a rash. The remedy for all these was the same—Dr Clark the family physician and Mr Brown the Windsor apothecary recommended 'a dose'. 'Opening medicine' was the panacea for all ills. The nursery cupboard was never without its bottle of castor oil (ordered weekly by Lady Lyttelton for safety's sake) and packets of Gray's powder, used for soothing upset stomachs: 'the Princess Royal although quite well in every other respect has not gained appetite despite the dose'—no wonder!

Great attention was paid to diet. Compared with present-day infant feeding it seems to fall short on protein, for there was a widespread fallacy that meat was dangerous and overheated the blood, but on the whole the royal children seemed to thrive well enough on their starch and milk. Vicky's appetite was fitful, she was too easily distracted and if at all out of sorts would lose interest in food altogether. On the other hand Bertie and Alice were hard to satisfy—they were always hungry and cried for more. There is a gentle hint in the reports that Dr Clark is partly to blame; he interfered too much, altered the regime too often, one day ordering cows' milk thickened with rusk and a little cream and sugar, but changing the next to asses' milk with rice (rusks to be eaten dry, only barley water to drink), so that the children never got used to a taste. Chicken broth, or mutton broth with a little meat, was given according to his whims and not the children's digestion. Later on boiled beef and carrots was often served, followed by a plain rice or semolina pudding. New nursery-maids were astonished by the simple food, and Mary Jones from Wales remarked that her family at home ate better; she 'never would have believed it if she had not seen it for herself'. Now and again Lady Lyttelton took matters into her own hands as the mother of five. If one of her charges became too obstreperous and unmanageable she cut out red meat for a day 'to cool them down'.

The royal children were not easily controlled. With the exception of Arthur, they were not naturally obedient either, for all were high-spirited. Although Vicky perfectly understood that she must not run out alone onto the terrace when staying in George IV's Pavilion at Brighton, a place not meant for children, she defied orders and almost fell through the balustrade, so that the distracted governess was forced to order the terrace to be wired in like a cage. How could she explain to so young a child that obedience was essential? All the children hated to be opposed, and tears and tantrums were a frequent occurrence. Vicky was highly intelligent, easily got bored with routine, and wanted to try her hand at more difficult things. Her tempers were a direct result of frustration. But how to keep her amused and yet not overstrain her?—the perpetual question of those in charge of clever children. Battles to be allowed to do more often ended in screams: 'I carried her sobbing to her room and put her to bed where she slept for an hour'; so ran the Lyttelton journal when Vicky was two-and-a-half. Alice too hated to be made to obey; when ordered to return a book she had taken from her brother, she instantly 'threw herself on the floor, striking her own face'.

The Prince of Wales's rages defied all description. His temper was unreliable, his screams when opposed so piercing that he became a disruptive influence in the nursery. His trouble was the exact opposite of Vicky's, nothing at all seemed to interest him, he could concentrate on nothing. Even peaceful mornings on the beach at Osborne could be ruined by Bertie's ill humour, but there, in the open air, the culprit could be dealt with promptly: 'after some hard digging and running about afterwards the Prince was too tired to scream'. Tantrums in the confined space of a nursery could not be controlled with quite the same happy results. When lessons were in progress, Bertie would 'dive under the table, upsetting the books and indulge in other anti-studious practices'. Lady Lyttelton knew that she ought to punish him for pulling his sisters' hair, scratching their faces, and snatching their toys, but would punishment make him any better? In her heart she did not believe in punishment, and in 1842 with the royal children in mind she wrote explaining her views to her daughter-in-law: 'I own I am against punishments, they wear out so soon and one is never sure they are fully understood by the child as belonging to the naughtiness. Besides children's memories are so short, the effect wears out so quickly.' To turn a blind eye might be all right in theory, but in practice it would not do. At one time Vicky started telling deliberate untruths—'a very serious offence indeed'. She coolly informed Mlle Charrier that 'Laddle' had given her permission to wear her pink bonnet for her outing, which was not so at all. When found out, she was 'imprisoned with tied hands and severely admonished and I trust was aware of her fault in the right way'. This sounds somewhat harsh, but the tender heart of the governess would not have allowed the hands to have been tied tightly, for Vicky was not at all cast down when her solitary confinement ended. Again for general naughtiness and persistent screams Alice received 'a sound whipping', although this was probably no more in fact than a sharp smack. But of all the punishments tried by the governess, the most effective of all was the loss of a 'treat'. To be deprived of dinner or a carriage drive with their mother, to be denied a walk or ride with their father 'had the desired effect and soon brought promises to be good'.

Lady Lyttelton's calm handling of the children, her reassuring manner and her motherliness, all had an excellent effect on Victoria and Albert, making them more tolerant towards their children, once they were less anxious and less weighed down by responsibility. They never ceased to be thankful that they had found someone older and wiser than they were and one whom they could trust to share the burden.

In one way the coming of the children precipitated the reorganisation of the dirty kitchen quarters and the overhaul of the unhealthy drainage system at Buckingham Palace and Windsor, which astonishingly enough had been neglected for centuries (bad drains were one of the greatest hazards to health in the nineteenth century). Since coming to England, Albert (who after living in rural Coburg had not acquired the Queen's immunity) had suffered from perpetual stomach upsets, sore throats and swollen glands, a direct result of this neglect. Typhoid and diphtheria, two infectious diseases that swept away many a young child, frequently started in the kitchen quarters, and Victoria and Albert soon began to realise that if they wished to have healthy children they must make a clean sweep here too. In consequence, they never had to go through the agony of losing a child (living in more backward countries Vicky lost two sons and Alice a son and a daughter, tragedies that they never got over). Their parents' assiduous care did have good results: all the royal children had healthy hair, good teeth and excellent complexions, not one suffered from bandy legs or rickets, malformations that disfigured many a child in those days.

It was fortunate that before the children grew up Osborne House and Balmoral were built, both on modern lines with a proper sewage system, plenty of lavatories and bathrooms, running hot and cold water (a novelty in those days) for family and servants alike. The children spent so much time in these holiday homes that they escaped many of the normal illnesses of childhood. The only two infectious diseases recorded are measles in 1853 and a mild form of scarlet fever in 1855. Even the common cold attacked them less frequently, although as a baby Bertie was never without a running nose. Both parents attributed this to the sea air and sea bathing at Osborne and the immunity derived from the 'hardening effect of the salt on the constitution'. When at Ramsgate as a child, Victoria had never bathed, and Coburg was so far from the coast that Albert had not even seen the sea until he visited his uncle in Belgium when he was in his teens, but both had great faith in its therapeutic properties. After the difficult and dangerous birth of Vicky's first child, her father begged her to come to Osborne for 'health-giving sea bathes', that would hasten her recovery. All the children learned to swim, even the baby was carried in for 'a dip', and if Queen Victoria preferred to bob up and down on the edge of the waves vigorously splashing sea water on face and arms, at least she had the satisfaction of thinking that it was doing her good.

The nursery itself was run on spartan lines—cold baths, open windows all the year round and small fires, for the germs of consumption were said not to flourish in a low temperature. Queen Victoria hated heat and she liked to say that all her children took after her (although in fact Vicky suffered from painful chilblains and every winter Alice and Beatrice were racked with rheumatism), while all the Queen's Court suffered agonies from the chill of Balmoral, especially after Albert's death. How Lady Lyttelton stood these hard conditions is difficult to say since she never complained, but at least she was able to creep away to her own warm room with its roaring fire and revive her frozen limbs: 'Fires are the peculiar blessing of one's own room', she said.

In two years (1842–1844) Lady Lyttelton's charges had doubled in number and there were now four babies under her care. Nightly she prayed with much humility to be given guidance to bring them up to choose the right path when confronted with temptation. Her aims for them were simple and unambitious: always to tell the truth; to be unselfish, obedient and loyal; to love their Father in Heaven, their parents and each other. She was a fervent believer in the power of prayer and prayed so often with the children that in consequence they were not at all self-conscious about dropping on their knees to give thanks for having been saved from an accident or for a blessing received.

Victoria and Albert felt it their duty to influence their children's religious beliefs and scorned to follow the new fashion which let children decide for themselves when they grew up. They took pains to present their opinions in a careful and straightforward way which would neither perplex nor alarm. Queen Victoria's memorandum on the religious training of children is a good example of how they set about this:

It is quite certain she should have a great reverence for God and for religion but that she should have the feeling of devotion and love which our heavenly Father encourages his earthly children to have for Him, and not one of fear and trembling, and the thought of death and an after life should not be represented in a forbidding and alarming way, and that she should be made to know as yet no difference of creeds, and not think that she can only pray on her knees and that those who do not kneel are less fervent or devout in their prayers.

Victoria believed that their mother should give children their first lesson in religion, which 'is best given to a child day by day at its mother's knee'. But it was not long after Vicky's birth that she began to realise that a Queen's many duties made it impossible for her to do this regularly. 'It is already a hard case for me,' she wrote in 1843, 'that my occupations prevent me being with her when she says her prayers.'

On the whole Queen Victoria's religious views were simple and straightforward. She felt it her duty to follow a middle course herself so as to avoid giving offence, although in practice she was a Low Church Anglican with a leaning towards Presbyterianism. But she showed a remarkably wide tolerance towards her Roman Catholic subjects and made a point of including some of them in her household if they were otherwise suitable—for instance, some members of the Catholic Howard family served her faithfully for many years. On the other hand, everyone knew that her favourite preacher was the Scottish Presbyterian divine Dr Macleod, whose sermons she kept by her and often quoted.

Albert's religious opinions were more complicated. He was brought up as a Lutheran, but not quite according to the pattern normal in Germany, for he had been much influenced in youth by his father's robustly liberal-minded chaplain Pastor Genzler. Contrary to the temper of the times, Genzler preached tolerance towards all faiths, the non-Christian included, and hated religious persecution. Albert brought with him from Germany the custom of taking Holy Communion only three times a year (at Christmas, Easter and Whitsun) and the Queen accepted this as right and proper. For twenty-four hours beforehand they would both withdraw from ordinary life and remain together in their room, reading, listening to sacred music and discussing religion, as well as praying for guidance in their own and their children's lives, thus putting themselves into a properly receptive frame of mind to take Holy Communion next day.

The English habit of kneeling in prayer was alien to Albert because of his Lutheran upbringing. He taught his children that there was no significance in the posture they adopted so long as they prayed with sincerity for strength to live according to the principles in which they believed. Yet Albert never once clashed with Lady Lyttelton on this point but allowed his children to kneel when they were with her without making an issue of it.

Very few directions were given to the governess by her royal employers, who had perfect trust in her judgement and good sense —save one: any sign of pride in the children must always be checked at once. They felt strongly about this. The children must never think that because of an accident of birth they belonged to a different and better species than others; therefore undue attention must never be paid to their special position. Haughtiness and a refusal to take the good with the bad were dealt with promptly and sharply. A fuss about having to wash their faces in cold water was countered by the reminder that the poor never washed in anything else. If they grumbled that they had no bedroom of their own, they were told they were lucky not to live in a slum where they would have to share with several brothers and sisters.

Rudeness to servants was always punished. Servants must not be overworked, asked to do the impossible, kept up late or treated with lack of consideration. Discovering one day that Bertie had belaboured his valet, Albert was far more angry than if he had struck a friend. Similarly the Queen banished a young Hohenzollern to her room for refusing to shake hands with John Brown. In 1844 Queen Victoria put their views on this point into a short memorandum. It ends thus: 'the greatest maxim of all is that the children should be brought up as simply and in as domestic a way as possible that (not interfering with their lessons) they should be as much as possible with their parents and learn to place the greatest confidence in them in all things.' As they decided in 1840 before their children began to arrive, good manners and consideration for others were best taught by example.

One of the most striking ways in which Albert shaped the family's life was his refusal to follow the standard English custom of the dreary Sunday which Victoria had always taken for granted. On the first Sunday after the honeymoon he had played chess with Stockmar as usual, and he kept the habit up. Once with a twinkle in his eye he got the sabbatarian Archdeacon Wilberforce into a tight corner by inviting him to take part in a game after he had preached the sermon at Windsor. However, all his efforts to enliven Sunday for the people were coldly received. Even though Queen Victoria backed her husband to the hilt, public opinion would not allow brass bands to play in the parks or the museums to be opened on Sundays—it smacked too much of foreign influence.

From their earliest days he insisted that his children should enjoy Sunday to the full. After Morning Service (and woe betide the clergyman who preached a long sermon—he was never asked again), and according to the season, they would skate, play battledore and shuttlecock in the long corridor at Windsor Castle, skittles on the lawn or take the dogs for an invigorating walk; every Sunday during the summer of 1851, Bertie recorded in his diary with monotonous regularity 'I sailed my yacht on the lake this afternoon'. The day often ended with Albert reading a chapter or two from a novel chosen by the Queen that could be enjoyed by them all, or there would be music and singing in one form or another. Victoria and Albert were not only conscientious parents, they were also young parents and therefore able to enter into their children's games with imagination and zest. Osborne

The Princess Royal (Vicky) in Turkish costume by Ross

Windsor Castle in Modern Times (detail) by Landseer

opened up a delightful sport which they could all share, even the latest baby—yachting. They enjoyed every moment of these 'marine excursions', as Queen Victoria called them, and every summer good weather would find them at sea either in the grand new *Victoria and Albert* or in the smaller steam yacht *Fairy*. Life on board was never dull—sketching, taking turns at sweeping the horizon with Albert's telescope, or pretending to steer. All rules were broken as the children romped on the deck dressed in smart sailor suits, making the most of the free-and-easy 'sailor-gypsy life' which Queen Victoria described in ecstatic terms to King Leopold of the Belgians. If the long-suffering Lady Lyttelton grumbled about interruptions to lessons, she had to admit that the children returned to her care looking brown and well.

In quite a different way Balmoral too held them all enthralled. The wonderfully fresh and sharp air gave them energy and kept everyone in the best of spirits, strong enough to enjoy long pony expeditions into the hills for a whole day at a time, their luncheon-baskets stuffed with enough food to satisfy ravenous appetites. There would be more sketching for the Queen and her daughters, deer-stalking and shooting for Albert and the boys, botanical explorations amongst the caves on the coast, Highland games to attend and at home reels every night, danced to the bagpipes.

Lady Lyttelton's correspondence tells us a great deal about Albert in the role of father. Since it was entirely his inspiration behind much that made life for the Queen and her children happy and carefree, it is extraordinary that he should ever have been looked on as a stern parent. Thirty years ago Mr Roger Fulford wrote that Albert, 'treated his children as intelligent human beings, with the dignity to which they were entitled, avoiding the boisterous chaff—crushing to youthful spirits—with which King Edward VII was to treat his own offspring. . . .' But no one wanted to believe this, and later writers have continued to label Albert as the wicked Victorian father. Yet in fact it was Bertie (Edward VII) who was often quite brutal to his children. The characters of father and son have in fact been reversed and the culprit has become the

victim. But Lady Lyttelton saw Albert as patient and good-
tempered when he played unselfconsciously with his children, and
her heart was touched at the way they looked up to him with love
and admiration. He seemed to understand instinctively how to
handle them and never pushed them beyond their capabilities. She
writes of Albert dragging them in turn round the nursery floor in a
basket to the accompaniment of shrieks of delight, or building a
house of bricks so tall that he had to stand on a chair to finish the
roof, watched all the while by a breathless audience. He taught
them to sing nursery rhymes, a child on each knee, the rest
clustered round, and somehow managed to keep his voice low
enough not to drown their thin high pipe. In her journal Queen
Victoria writes of Albert playing hide and seek with Vicky and
Bertie with the dash and gusto of a boy, turning somersaults on a
haystack 'to show Bertie how to do it', or noisily and eagerly
managing a new kite on a windy day at Osborne. 'He is so kind to
them', she wrote, 'romps with them so delightfully and manages
them so beautifully and firmly.'

In a letter to his stepmother, Albert himself describes a happy
and peaceful summer day at Osborne which speaks of contentment
and family harmony: the Queen resting under a tree with a book
in her hand, the children waiting to march off with their father,
armed with butterfly-nets and jam-jars. The children were fortunate in having parents who were young, full of zest and vigour,
adventurous yet dependable and kind. When they were playing
with their father and the Queen ran to join them, in a simple dress
and with hair down her back, it was difficult to tell mother and
children apart. Victoria now enjoyed with her family all the fun
she had missed in her own childhood. The card-tricks Albert
devised, the magic he pretended to perform, thrilled her as much
as it did the children. When he read aloud to them of an evening,
it was round the Queen's sofa that they gathered, Albert's chair
drawn up alongside. It was such a perfect family group that it is a
great pity that Winterhalter did not record it for posterity instead
of one of his more formal poses.

1

Victoria

'A child of very strong feelings'

VICTORIA AND ALBERT's first child arrived on 21 November 1840. The announcement of the birth of a Princess Royal caused no dismay in the country at large; England was reasonably content under a female sovereign. But her sex did give Vicky's father a momentary pang of disappointment which lasted only until Mrs Lilley the mid-wife put the baby into his arms. From that moment there awoke in the young father a deep feeling of love and tenderness for the child, the first thing in his adopted country that was really his own, and he had to turn away to hide his emotion.

The birth was not nearly so painful as the Queen had feared—which was just as well since she was to go through the performance eight times more. Her recovery was rapid and she was able to enjoy her child from the first; but perhaps it would be truer to say that it gave her great pleasure to watch her husband enjoying their child because, as she told King Leopold with her usual honesty, 'he makes a capital nurse which I do not'.

On one point the Queen would not be moved. She obstinately refused to feed the child herself, showing a disgust for that natural function so deep-seated that she would not listen to Albert's entreaties. The duchess of Kent had had no inhibitions about this; she had nursed Victoria for a full nine months, with great benefit to the child, so the Queen did not get her revulsion (for it amounted to that) from her mother. It is very probable that Victoria's governess Louise Lehzen, a jealous and possessive spinster with thwarted maternal feelings, had turned her against breast feeding. Lehzen could have told the Queen of the old wives' tale (believed by the ignorant and superstitious in backward parts of Germany) that hereditary taints are passed on through the mother's milk. A wet nurse was engaged but she had such a taste for cheese and beer that the baby suffered from colic and wailed persistently. Dr Clark ordered soothing medicine which after the custom of the times contained laudanum, a drug that made her pale and lethargic. Nor did Pussy (as Albert called his daughter) take kindly to weaning. The change of diet caused her to lose weight, so in order to put some fat on her Dr Clark ordered cream in her cereal, butter on her rusks and rich mutton broth—with the natural result that she became sicker, paler and thinner than ever, and her father distracted with worry. He feared that they were going to lose her just as Queen Adelaide, wife of the previous King, William IV, had lost all her little girls; nothing definite had been wrong with them, they had simply faded away.

There was more to the baby's health than diet. Despite endless confabulations with Stockmar before the Queen's confinement, nothing in the nursery was quite right. This was partly Stockmar's own fault; having laid down rules for the management of the baby and the nurses, he did not stay long enough to see that they were carried out but left London for Coburg as soon as he knew the Queen was out of danger. The main trouble sprang from the lack of co-operation between Mrs Southey, the Lady Superintendent, and the chief nurse Mrs Roberts. No one was really in charge. Mrs Southey was a weak and ineffective woman much taken up with her own imaginary ailments and was often to be found wrapped in shawls, toasting her toes by a roaring fire in a hot and airless nursery with all the windows shut. Stockmar as a former practising doctor had strictly forbidden this, knowing that such temperatures encouraged germs and sickness.

Albert and Mrs Roberts were barely on speaking terms. It was impossible not to sense his hostility and his disapproval of her friendship with Lehzen, who since the Queen's accession had been raised to the rank of Lady Companion with the title of Baroness. It seemed to Albert that Lehzen was always in the nursery, often with the baby on her lap when she should be in her cot asleep or out of doors in the fresh air. He spoke sharply to Mrs Roberts about this and she much resented his interference, marching off to complain to the Queen that the Prince was blaming her because the child was not thriving. Matters went from bad to worse and on his return from Coburg, Stockmar was dismayed to find the nursery in chaos, the baby ailing, Albert distraught and at odds with the Queen who had taken the nurses' side. Stockmar's solution was drastic—out they had to go. As with the kitchens a little later on, he and Albert reorganised the nursery from top to bottom. Lady Lyttelton took Mrs Southey's place, sensible and motherly Mrs Sly replaced Mrs Roberts. There was another important change which had far-reaching consequences for Albert. He persuaded Victoria to pension off Lehzen, the real cause of the trouble, and send her back to her native Germany. On 23 September 1842 the Baroness left England never to return. Before long, Lady Lyttelton's experienced eye had spotted the trouble with Pussy: she was being given too rich a diet; instant improvement followed when she was given plainer and more wholesome food. Albert now became a welcome visitor to the nursery, indeed possibly the most important single factor for the successful up-bringing of the children was the mutual respect that quickly blossomed into affection between Albert and Lady Lyttelton; it endured without a single shadow until her retirement eight years later.

Theorising in the style of those lengthy memoranda of 1840 had not stopped with the Princess Royal's birth. Both the young parents had decided that the baby must be kept away from the court in case she should become spoiled and get an inflated idea of her position. This was managed so effectively that Vicky was eight months old before Lady Lyttelton (still the Queen's Woman of the Bedchamber at that time) chanced to see her. Lady Lyttelton was amused when she later heard the reason for the seclusion, for she had noticed at once that Albert spoiled and petted his child outrageously, adoring her unashamedly even in front of strangers. Victoria and Albert were too inexperienced to understand that if no one saw the child rumours would begin to circulate; it took years to dispel the gossip that Vicky was blind, deaf and dumb, even imbecile. The royal response was to swing to the other extreme: everyone who came to Buckingham Palace and Windsor Castle had to see and admire this perfection of babyhood. Albert gloried in the praise showered on her bright complexion, fair curly hair and enormous intelligent eyes of the deepest blue. Very quickly the child learned to speak with great fluency, distracting her mother when she should have been concentrating on state papers, while ministers had to put up with her crawling under their feet and pulling herself up by their trouser-legs.

Soon Vicky was meeting everyone as a matter of course; she quickly showed her preferences. The ungainly Czar of Russia became her favourite at once, in spite of the rolling eyes and harsh laugh which were enough to scare the wits out of any child. She sat happily on his knee sucking a huge bloodstone that hung from his watch chain. Another favourite was the duke of Wellington who treated the child like an adult, bowing low and kissing her hand. Louis Philippe, though the father of many children, frightened her with his high-pitched voice and excitable ways. The cold, formal manners of the Hohenzollerns in their turn made a bad impression only equalled by the unsympathetic natures of the Queen's uncles, who invariably called when Lady Lyttelton had got the child contentedly settled, stared at her provokingly until she burst into tears and vexed the Queen very much with their criticism: 'How very odd, my daughters never did cry!'

It was fortunate that Lady Lyttelton understood from the first how to handle her charge, for Vicky's mercurial temperament made her the very antithesis of the typical obedient nineteenth-century child. She would roar with rage one moment and be all smiles and contrition the next; she was defiant when bored or frustrated, yet showed an honesty that never failed to appeal. But Lady Lyttelton noticed that these strong feelings hid a sensitive heart which could be deeply wounded and that it would be a mistake to think her self-centred because she had charm and easily got her own way. Her mind was so advanced for her age that it was hard to keep her suitably occupied without overtaxing her, and still more difficult to keep up with her demands.

Her fond governess could not resist the temptation of recording the child's clever remarks which she called 'malicious and sly', meaning that they were sharp and very much to the point. At the age of three, when out riding with her French governess Mlle Charrier, she made it plain that she perfectly understood a verse of Lamartine's, for when they stopped to watch some sheep and cows peacefully grazing in a field she exclaimed 'Voilà le tableau qui se déroule à mes pieds'. The delighted Queen passed on many of these stories of her eldest's genius to her long-suffering Uncle Leopold who could not help smiling to see his niece so enthralled where once she had seemed so indifferent, and feared that the child might be ruined by such doting parents. Stockmar was of that opinion too, although he adored with the rest and thought the princess exceptional; when she was a little older he told King Leopold that an appeal to her good sense never failed and that she was far too warm and affectionate to hurt anyone knowingly.

All too soon the baby turned into a neat-fingered talkative little girl who was always busy. At four years old with her maid Aimée to guide her, Vicky to her own great delight did a great many 'stitches of cross-stitch on coarse canvas with a large blunt needle'. The year before, she had suddenly refused to eat her dinner with a spoon, demanded a fork and managed it perfectly. At six she progressed from painting daubs on large sheets of paper to proper drawing lessons at her own request. Drawing and painting were always to be her greatest recreation, even more than music at which she also showed talent. She learned to read easily without being specially taught; Lady Lyttelton discovered this by chance one day soon after her fourth birthday, when the child brought her a book she was looking at to have a difficult word explained. Having once been given an explanation she never forgot it, and she lapped up knowledge with an ease that was almost alarming; her governess found it difficult to keep pace with her progress and said only half in jest that she would soon have to go back to school again herself. The household solemnly declared that she was so forward that she must surely be burnt out by the time she was twenty. Albert and Lady Lyttelton knew better. In their opinion all the signs pointed to her becoming a highly intelligent but very normal woman. She had a strongly-marked maternal instinct and loved playing with dolls, for instance (she owned a considerable number, though not nearly as many as her mother, for she had no need of substitute brothers and sisters). As happens in all large families, Vicky and the other children made many of their own amusements. They all preferred digging on the sands at Osborne to looking after the individual gardens which had been allotted them, but in later life Vicky inherited her father's green fingers and his flair for planning a garden, demonstrating it when she restored the once beautiful grounds of the Neue Palais in Potsdam and planted trees and shrubs in the uncultivated land around her castle at Kronberg.

Vicky loved to be out of doors in all weathers; rain or snow made no difference, for she bloomed in the fresh air. It was only when, after her marriage, she had to live in overheated rooms made fetid by smoking that she drooped and felt unwell. Brisk exercise out of doors (like an early morning ride with her husband) always restored her energy, but it was hard to find this in a great city like Berlin.

The sea played a large part in Vicky's young life. She saw it first at Brighton where Lady Lyttelton had taken her to recover from a cold. Before Osborne House was built George IV's extravagant Brighton pavilion was the only seaside home Victoria and Albert owned. The oriental opulence of the place prevented them from appreciating its beauty, but from the first Vicky adored it, loving the exotic atmosphere and the strong colours. The strange shape of much of the furniture held for her a perpetual interest and charm— and her extrovert nature and gregariousness responded to the crowds which thronged the streets surrounding the building, while for their part the populace pressing to catch a glimpse of this diminutive Royal Highness found her shrieks of delight a welcome change from the cold response of her parents to any invasion of their privacy. Later on, after her marriage, Osborne became a regular holiday refuge for tired and overstrained nerves. The equivalents in Germany were the crowded spas where it was fashionable for the well-known to congregate. Vicky found them detestable, and whenever she could obtain the King of Prussia's permission (which was not always forthcoming) brought her children to Osborne for fresh air and sea bathing.

Vicky could not remember a time when the royal nursery was empty of babies; there was even one in it (Beatrice) when she was married. Her brother Bertie (the Prince of Wales) was born before her first birthday, and so it went on until the birth of Beatrice in 1857. There was always a baby to nurse, a brother to fight, a sister to share secrets with. Vicky adored them all and gave them warmth and affection all her life, never once feeling jealousy or envy, the two emotions that break up family ties. From an early age she learned to share everything she possessed, and took it for granted that she had to be careful of her clothes since Alice was waiting for them. More remarkable, and a great tribute to the sweetness of her nature, was her acceptance of the fact that she must share her parents' love as well. She never really understood until she left home as a married woman how much her father's favourite she was, for he had always been fair, never singling one child out more than another, so that it seemed natural to her that her parents should love them all equally. Quite naturally too she developed early the sense of responsibility peculiar to the eldest child of a large family (especially if she is a girl). She accepted the burden as a privilege.

With a nursery filling fast, so many bedrooms were needed that Vicky had to share hers with Alice, two and a half years her junior. Alice soon became her bosom friend and boon companion, although made of frailer stuff than herself, as she instinctively recognised; years later she determinedly defended Alice when she was a target for the widowed Queen's ill-humour. It was a mark of her high principles that she never allowed the Queen to find fault with Alice without pointing out respectfully but firmly that her mother was in the wrong. She never forgot her father's insistence that she must not be afraid to speak the truth whatever the consequences.

In 1844 a clergyman's daughter, Sarah Anne Hildyard (the children called her 'Tilla'), joined the royal teaching staff. She was the daughter of one of Stockmar's clerical friends and proved a most suitable young woman. The Queen and Albert, interviewing her together, found her gentle (but not weak), modest, with a sense of humour and high principles. She had, too, a wide range of interests which included scientific subjects such as botany, of which she was almost as knowledgeable as Albert himself. As Albert told Stockmar, Sarah Hildyard was indeed a lucky find. Because Vicky was so precocious it was decided to start serious lessons before she was five, since 'keeping her back' was useless. Lady Lyttelton had been pressing for this, since she herself could teach the child no more; as she told her daughter-in-law, 'Princessy is beginning to try one's depth'. Vicky's fits of rage, she assured the Queen, were the result of boredom, not bad temper, and were cries for help which must be understood and answered. She was proved right when Vicky's response to real work was immediate. Miss Hildyard wanted to teach, and Vicky to learn, so they liked each other from the start. Moreover, it gave the child a feeling of importance to sit at a real desk in a real schoolroom with books, maps and a blackboard, the whole atmosphere redolent of learning; the total compatibility between governess and pupil made this atmosphere doubly effective, and Vicky responded enthusiastically.

Up to now the Queen had been reading an instructive book to Vicky whenever she had the time. She much enjoyed the quiet hours and they did something to satisfy her conscience for she believed that every mother should have a share in her daughter's education. But with Miss Hildyard's arrival she had to admit that she was beaten. It was disconcerting to have Vicky ask questions she could not answer, even more disconcerting to suspect that Vicky knew the answer already and was merely testing her mother's knowledge. However, it was thought wiser to allow the Queen still to give Vicky religious instruction.

In some ways Vicky was old for her age, but most nineteenth-century children matured early and were far more familiar with death and disease than we are today. Victoria and Albert were unusual in that they never knew the tragedy of losing a child (Vicky herself never completely recovered from the death of two young sons, nor Alice from the loss of a son and a daughter). Vicky remembered being frequently in and out of mourning ('my sad dress') for a relation or a public figure throughout her girlhood, and hated it. It was disconcerting, even frightening, to be made to change suddenly and without warning from her favourite blue or red into funereal black. Too often it was for someone she had never heard of, and because she was a child of spirit she did not hesitate to rebel. The only person for whom she willingly wore black was the duke of Wellington. Long before he died in 1852, she had come to believe that he had saved her mother's throne during the Chartist riots in 1848, when her own security had for the first time been badly shaken. The year of revolutions could have been hilarious fun for a girl less sensitive than Vicky, for Buckingham Palace was filled to the roof with children of her own age who had fled with their parents to the safety of England from disaster abroad. But she had seen her mother weep and her father wring his hands in anguish at the fate which had overtaken so many crowned heads, so when the duke died she willingly put on her black dress and, wearing a bracelet with a medallion containing a lock of the old man's hair, went off with the Queen to his lying-in-state at Chelsea hospital and burst into tears when she saw his coffin.

The trials and tribulations suffered by her parents were all part of her life: the unexpected fall of a congenial government, the treachery of a fellow monarch, the anguish of the Crimean war, the agony of the Indian mutiny. But hardest for a child to bear, because least understood, were the unjust accusations of pro-Russian sympathy hurled at her father during a wild period of xenophobia that gripped England in 1854. It was bewildering for Vicky to remember that three years earlier the Prince Consort's name had stood so high through the resounding success of the Great Exhibition. That loyalty was a difficult virtue she learned the hard way by noticing the unpopularity her father incurred when he championed Lord Canning, Governor-General of India, after he had refused to order cruel and indiscriminate punishment for the mutineers; but the lesson sank deep into her consciousness, for Albert's remark 'one brutality cannot wipe out another' was echoed fifteen years later by her during the Franco-Prussian war, 'A wounded man is not an enemy.'

To Vicky, her father was an oracle, the guiding star in her life, the one person to whom she could tell everything without fear of being misunderstood. They complemented each other perfectly. If Albert felt depressed or weighed down with affairs of state, an hour of Vicky's company restored his good humour. 'You have his mind,' the Queen wrote to her only a few days after Albert's death and indeed her intellect was the only masculine thing about this essentially feminine girl. Her father's teaching during the years between fourteen and seventeen in preparation for her marriage (to enable her to be a real help to her husband when he succeeded to the throne of Prussia), turned her from a clever child into a most accomplished young woman. Politics, philosophy, history, the literature of England, France and Germany, were gone into with great thoroughness, yet there was still time for lessons from such distinguished men as Faraday, who became her friend. She read widely, and her reading did not stop with marriage. Despite her many duties as wife, mother and princess, her programme of study was formidable. In her first year in Prussia apart from English and French journals, novels, biographies and travel books sent out from Mudie's in London, she tackled de Tocqueville, Aeschylus and Euripides as well as Motley's *Rise of the Dutch Republic*. She read Darwin's *Origin of Species* as soon as it was published and was the first member of the royal family to read Karl Marx and to take an interest in the new subject of psychology. Yet she never thought of herself as clever or particularly outstanding in any way—that was a great part of her charm.

Love came early to Vicky. She became secretly engaged to Prince Frederick William, heir presumptive to the King of Prussia, when she was only fourteen. They first met when he came to England in 1851 for the Great Exhibition and stayed at Buckingham Palace. Marriage was not thought of then, for she was only ten, but three years later Fritz came again, proposed to Vicky in the hills above Balmoral, and was accepted. It was an arranged marriage, but Victoria and Albert would never have pressed for it if there had not been love. Despite the agony of parting from her parents at the age of seventeen to live hundreds of miles away with a husband who was still partly a stranger, Vicky always described her marriage as 'my golden lot'.

2

Albert Edward

'He shows great quickness and power of
learning but is unaccountably averse to it'

───────────────

'THE NEXT WILL be a Prince.' The Queen's confident pronouncement after the birth of the Princess Royal was fulfilled on 9
November 1841, twelve days before Vicky's first birthday. It was
'much too soon', she told her eldest daughter years later, and she
suffered for it. Although she had an excellent pregnancy (a few
days before the confinement Lady Lyttelton had remarked on her
mistress's remarkable energy) and had gone into labour with far
more confidence than the first time, the birth was protracted and
difficult, her recovery so slow and painful that it left her suffering
from depression, sleeplessness and irritability.

Albert Edward was christened in St George's Chapel, Windsor,
and not (like Vicky) in the throne-room at Buckingham Palace,
because the press vociferously demanded that the baptism of the
heir to the throne should take place in public. The importance of
this child was not lost on Frederick William III of Prussia, who
readily accepted the Queen's invitation to be chief sponsor, much
to the satisfaction of parents eager for England to begin forging
links with Germany.

As an infant in arms the Prince of Wales (or 'the boy' as he was
called for a short time) gave little trouble. He was placid rather
than lively, slow to cut teeth, walk and talk. Unlike his elder
sister, whose complexion was rosy, he was pale with grey eyes
that sometimes looked almost blue, but his best feature was his
soft brown hair which became lighter in colour as he grew older.
Although small-boned like all the Queen's children, he was fatter
and rounder than Pussy and gave less trouble with his feeding.
From the moment of his birth parents and nurses doted on this

fair, blue-eyed baby. It can safely be said that he never knew what
it was not to be surrounded by love and warmth; the difficulty lay
in his inability to return it. The only one who did not care for him
was his sister Vicky, who screamed and refused to be pacified
when taken for a peep at the new occupant of a cradle that until
recently had been all hers. The reason for his lateness in talking
with any clarity did not become evident until after his second
birthday, when Dr Clark detected a slight impediment in his
speech. It was not exactly George III's stutter, although the child
did inherit that too in some small degree, but a real inability to
make himself understood. Although he never recovered completely from this, he did learn in time to speak reasonably well,
while the stutter disappeared altogether. This impediment caused
the guttural accent which is mentioned so frequently by his bio-
graphers who, however, explain it as the consequence of speaking
so much German to his parents. None of them has remembered that
the children spoke nothing but English at home, nor stopped to
inquire how a boy brought up to speak English with an English
nurse could acquire a German intonation. Wisely, Albert was
against drawing too much attention to this handicap and it was
largely due to his patience and commonsense that the child made
some improvement.

The parents' troubles with this boy were only just beginning: by
the time he could walk some of his behaviour began to cause real
anxiety. Violent rages racked him, often triggered off (or so it
seemed) by the most trivial incidents. Victoria and Albert told
each other that it was only a phase that he would grow out of, and
that they must not make too much of tantrums in such a young
child. They pointed to Vicky as an example; recently she had
shown a marked improvement and no doubt 'the boy' would too.
Unfortunately, as he grew stronger so did his temper, and he
would scream, kick and lash out at the nearest person, becoming
really difficult to control. Small though he was, it sometimes
needed two people to hold him in case he harmed himself or even
one of the other children with anything that lay to hand—perhaps

a pair of scissors from his nurse's work-box or a knife snatched from the table. Mrs Sly was so alarmed by these displays that she did everything possible to avoid a scene and gave in to him more than she should, with the result that he became worse instead of better. As he got older the 'fits' (as they began to be called by those who cared for him) lasted longer and took more out of him. He would scream, stamp his feet, tear his books, scratch and bite his sisters, frequently kicking them and pulling their hair until the nursery was filled with wails. Afterwards he would lie pale, panting and listless for hours, not understanding a word that was said to him. Dr Clark soothingly assured the parents that there was nothing to be alarmed about, but Stockmar's medical experience made him take a graver view and he advised Albert never to leave Bertie alone with the younger children. Lady Lyttelton had no more success with him than Mrs Sly. At four he could not concentrate at all, and when she tried to teach him his letters (an exercise which Vicky and Alice enjoyed very much) he would crawl under the table and refuse to come out. Far from showing anger, his governess found all sorts of excuses: Vicky's intelligence overshadowed him, perhaps she set too high a standard, they all expected too much, or he felt inferior because he was not as tall as Alice though nearly two years older. But in her heart Lady Lyttelton knew all this to be nonsense. True, Vicky teased Bertie for being slow, but this sort of thing was only normal between brother and sister, and she never bullied him. If she started on him first he immediately retaliated by pulling her hair and giving her a smart kick on the shins. It was always Vicky who cried.

There were moments of hope when Bertie was affectionate, even winning, and the family made more of these rare flashes of charm than perhaps they deserved, for in these moods he might play quite happily with the other children for a little while. But he could never be trusted not to round on the others suddenly and without reason; it was all very wearing for parents and governesses alike. Lady Lyttelton, who was no longer young, was often quite worn out since she had no experience of dealing with a highly-strung, excitable child who seemed to lack all sense of right and wrong.

Few outside the palace knew anything of the parents' difficulties, yet 'who shall educate the Prince of Wales' was freely discussed in the press, by the Church and by all those busybodies who think they have a right to interfere in the affairs of the royal family. It was only half in jest that Albert referred to his eldest son as the 'nation's child'. Both parents tried to keep a sense of humour at the interference they were forced to endure. In 1842 an anonymous pamphlet was published, full of weird and wild ideas and laying down the law on how the Prince of Wales should be educated. It was an immediate bestseller and was read at the palace, where some of the more reasonable points were noted. Stockmar put it into the fire. He advised Victoria and Albert to do the same with all the free advice they were given, telling them that since the Queen was so young (barely twenty-two) much would have altered before the boy became King, and it would be better to map out his education on broad principles only. In an age of profound changes it might be important to teach him to be adaptable and to have a flexible outlook: 'keeping as his keynote freedom of thought, the boy should be made aware of this in order to act as a balance wheel on the movements of the social body'. Stockmar then repeated his old warning: the only thing that really mattered was that the Prince of Wales's education should be English from start to finish. Even a year at a continental university (useful perhaps for the other children) would be quite out of place for him.

On one point, however, Stockmar was silent—the boy's inability to learn. Stockmar assumed of course that the Prince would be normally intelligent, and at the time he made this remark even Victoria and Albert scarcely dared face the cruel fact that he was not. Their chief anxiety was that he might not be able to continue and develop the social reforms which lay so near Albert's heart. By the time his son was ten Albert knew that Bertie would never be able to do this. Queen Victoria was more optimistic; surely Bertie could be made to see, as she had done herself, what a disgrace it was that more than half his subjects had not nearly enough to eat?

Albert's attitude to his eldest son has been much misunderstood and much criticised. Bertie is supposed to have been bullied and crushed by his father's harsh treatment and to have been under a permanent strain from too much work too rigidly demanded. The fits are explained as the consequences of stress and a lack of affection and understanding. The truth is quite different. Albert was an approachable, caring father, patient and kindly towards all his children alike, and he was certainly not so foolish as to defeat his own ends by forcing a child to work above his intellectual level. On the contrary, he did what every sensible parent would do—he modified the 'plan' to suit Bertie's mental capacity. For example, when he wrote that English and French were to be taught for one hour a day, he of course knew that French would not be the same chore to Bertie as to the average schoolboy, for he had been speaking it from babyhood, but this simple fact is often overlooked. Again, to answer questions about a story that had been read aloud or to reproduce the narrative was surely not very difficult for a child of eight? A tired child cannot concentrate, and Albert realised that since Bertie had difficulty in concentrating at all times it was specially important to keep him fresh if he was to learn anything at all, and this is why he arranged for a 'difficult lesson', such as English or arithmetic, to be followed by music, drawing or a story. Albert wrote: 'It will be well to let mental and mere mechanical exertion alternate in order not to strain the intellect or exhaust the patience of the child. Immediately after the meal in the middle of the day it will be well not to work the mind of the child.'

Another surprise to many was Albert's attitude to church-going for his children. Bertie was 'not to go to church until after his eighth birthday, although a short doctrinal exercise might be read by the tutor'. The boy himself corroborates this in his diaries, for he writes under November 1850 (when he was nine): 'Organists Festival at St Georges's Chapel with Papa and Vicky. It was the first time I had been to church in public.' This might shock the pious, but was unquestionably right for Bertie. It is also another instance to prove that his parents were against making the boy do something he could not understand. The public were critical of Albert on another count too—that he did not wish to appoint a clergyman as tutor. How astonished they would have been had they known that Albert's reason was the very human one that a clergyman might think it his duty to spoil Bertie's pleasure on Sundays, whereas the Queen and Albert believed strongly that Sunday should be a day of fun and relaxation! What a furore it would have caused had it become known that the royal parents allowed, even encouraged, amateur theatricals as well as the reading of novels on the sabbath, as well as other innocent amusements not permitted in many Christian homes. Albert intended the day to stand out from all others and to be looked forward to with pleasurable anticipation rather than dreaded for its solemnity and gloom.

The Prince of Wales was not isolated from his parents; Albert took the boy with him as much as possible. In 1847 Bertie writes that he went deer-stalking and shooting with his father in Scotland, a sport he seems to have much enjoyed. After 1854 he several times mentions playing hockey at Windsor 'with Papa and several others'—so he was not excluded from any general fun that was going. In 1849 he was given his first gun, specially made for an eight-year-old to handle (the same gun that Grant, the head keeper at Balmoral, later used to teach Prince William of Prussia how to shoot although he had a withered hand). It was a birthday present, and as children do Bertie made a list of his other presents which included 'a microscope, a seal, a box of experiments and some fine picture books'. The 'fine picture-books' are worth noting—given in the hope, perhaps, of improving the knowledge and awakening the interest of a backward child. The entry in Bertie's diary is a little longer than usual on this particular birthday, for after the list of presents he adds: 'Several Eton boys came to tea and stayed until 7.30.' Bertie's diary makes nonsense of the theory, still widely believed, that he was a lonely boy who was never allowed play-mates, for there are many similar entries. He seems in fact to have had a wide circle of friends of his own age who came regularly to play with him and his brother Alfred. Possibly because he was unimaginative and could not think of much else to say, he kept merely factual records of these visits. 'Treats' are often mentioned: a pantomime, a children's dance, a visit by Astley's acrobats and a menagerie. 'I stayed up until 12.30', he wrote exultantly in November 1855, presumably after one of the dances; like his mother, he always loved dancing, especially Scottish reels. There is record, too, of visits to the Crystal Palace in Hyde Park while the huge glass structure was rising like a mushroom from the earth, sometimes with his father and some-times with his tutor, and there can be no doubt that he found these breaks in routine great fun. On the opening day of the Great Exhibition he derived tremendous satisfaction from the admiring glances cast in his direction as he walked beside his mother resplendent in his kilt—he was always to love dressing up.

In 1854 Bertie was taught to swim by an Eton boatman. As soon as he was proficient enough for Albert to be confident that he would not drown, he was allowed to swim in the Thames every summer the family were at Windsor and was taken by his father on 'marine excursions' in the royal steam yacht *Fairy* to the west coast of Scotland to look for botanical specimens. Clad in mackintosh and boots and armed with torches, they spent hours searching the rocks while Albert kept his son interested with a running com-mentary on what they were looking for and why. Yet there is not one word in Bertie's diary to suggest that he found these trips (which would have held an air of mystery and adventure for most boys) in the least enjoyable, just a flat statement that they had taken place and that his brother had been one of the party. Albert must have suffered more than one pang of disappointment that

Bertie showed so little interest in what would have been the height
of excitement for him at the same age.

When Bertie was seven years old he was taken out of Lady
Lyttelton's care and handed over to Miss Hildyard for more
advanced work in the schoolroom which had been set up for
Vicky and where Alice too was already busy with regular lessons.
At about the same time he started music with Mrs Anderson (who
taught all the children for some years), but much to her own
chagrin she entirely failed to teach him a note. Miss Hildyard
continued to have a hand in his education for the next two or three
years although a tutor was appointed for him in 1849, when he was
barely eight. Therefore it is simply untrue to say, as is so often
done, that Bertie was abruptly snatched out of the care of women
and handed over to the exclusive charge of men at the tender age
of seven.

The new tutor was Henry Birch, a young man still under thirty
who had been popular at Cambridge and a great success as a master
at Eton. Not unnaturally Albert was highly delighted at securing
such a prize. He had been long enough in England to know that
good tutors were rare and difficult to find, because of the English
system of education where a tutor was usually employed merely to
get a boy into public school and not, as on the continent, instead of
school itself.

One of the things Albert liked about Birch was his clear voice
and beautiful pronunciation; he had none of those habits Albert
found so irritating—mumbling, putting his hand over his mouth
when speaking or talking too quietly. These were qualities
essential in the man who had to teach the heir to the throne to
speak clearly.

With relief Albert noticed when he warned Birch about Bertie's
irrational rages that the young tutor took the news in his stride and
was in no way put out. After much consultation, the two men
decided that a modified form of the 'plan' should be tried for the
first year at least. For instance Latin was not to be taught until the

boy was older; according to Bertie himself it was begun on 2 January 1852—'yesterday I commenced learning Latin'. At ten he was four years older than his sister Vicky or his father and uncle had been when they started. Teaching the heir to the throne soon became uphill work for Birch, a pleasant ordinary man used to ordinary boys who found his pupil's inattention and naughtiness hard to bear. Remembering his successful Eton days he tried the effect of a little chaff, but soon discovered to his cost that it would not do, and suggested that competition might stimulate his pupil; Albert then agreed to allow Alfred (Affie) to join in Bertie's lessons. Although three years younger, Affie was bright as a button, enjoyed hard work and showed no lack of concentration or boredom. There was a slight improvement in Bertie after this, although he still remained as excitable and strange as ever. This was particularly evident in his obsession with sticks of all kinds. Whenever he went for a walk with his tutor he would continually dart away to search for them. They had to be of one particular 'whippy' kind that made a cutting sound when he whirled them above his head. When he found just what he was looking for he would run on ahead, excitedly begin hitting a tree or a gate, or would lunge suddenly at the tutor himself, listening to the sound the stick made with a look of pleasure. Bertie took great delight in his collection of sticks and early in his tutorship Henry Birch saw the danger to life and limb and took them away, but the scene that followed was so awful that thereafter he took the line of least resistance and let the boy keep them.

In 1852 Mr Birch resigned. He had been tutor to the Prince of Wales for over two years—two of the longest years of his life. He left the royal service suffering from exhaustion, low spirits and lack of sleep, but he realised that if he stayed much longer his career in the Church—postponed at Victoria and Albert's request —would be in ruins. Queen Victoria especially was vexed that Bertie had made so little progress and was inclined to blame the tutor, but with her usual fairness she blamed herself too, because Bertie had inherited her aversion to scholars: 'to say the honest truth', she wrote to Vicky in 1859, 'the sight of a professor or a learned man alarms me and is not sympathetic to me . . . you can see why Bertie dislikes them. He is my caricature, that is my misfortune and in a man this is much worse.' Stockmar most unfairly echoed these sentiments with 'He is an exaggerated copy of his mother.' Bertie could be sharp enough if he wished, but there is no doubt that he had a stubborn resistance to learning that was impossible to overcome.

Even as early as 1852 the good looks praised by Lady Lyttelton had begun to disappear. Pale and languid, he became a constant source of worry. Unfortunately, the fact that Dr Clark found nothing wrong did not mean that all was well, for Bertie would hang his head and not answer when spoken to and seemed to take no interest in anything. Since he was small for his age, the Queen could not use the excuse that he was outgrowing his strength, nor could she suggest that his failure to grow was the consequence of any over-rigorous system of learning. Lethargy slowed down his progress in the schoolroom so much that in a fit of exasperation Albert exclaimed that at least he must be taught enough to be able to read and write and make a reasonable speech, and even began to doubt whether it would ever be possible to teach him at all.

Frederick Weymouth Gibbs was chosen to succeed Henry Birch. He had been recommended to Albert by Sir James Stephen, Regius Professor of History at Cambridge, who had brought Gibbs up and thought him just right for the job. It is surprising that such a very clever young man, a fellow of Trinity College, Cambridge and a barrister, could have been persuaded to accept the post, even at the large salary of £1000 a year. But it is possible that he was pressed into doing so by Sir James Stephen to whom he owed a debt of gratitude for taking him into his household.

An aura of sadism has always hung about the name of Frederick Weymouth Gibbs, who has been regularly accused of a strictness towards his pupil which amounted to cruelty, while Bertie has won much sympathy for the unhappiness he is supposed to have endured at Gibbs' hands. In fact Gibbs was a shy, retiring man who would not hurt a fly, but like most shy men he found it necessary to take on a protective covering of sternness and hauteur in public. The legend of cruelty has grown and gathered momentum on the flimsy basis of Gibbs' sad family history—his father was a bankrupt and his mother died in an asylum. During the whole time he was tutor to the heir to the throne, Bertie made his life a torment, and so far from being the persecutor Gibbs was in fact the persecuted. He left royal service in the end simply to prevent himself from becoming a physical and mental wreck, and his diary tells of the sufferings he endured from Bertie's unpredictable temper and the attacks upon him. 'He has thrown dirt and swung a large stick at me', runs one entry; 'he struck me with a large stick in a passion' runs another, followed by 'The Prince told me not to allow this, that if he did so I must box his ears and take the same stick and rap his knuckles sharply.'

A few months later Frederick Gibbs wrote:

I had to do some arithmetic with the Prince of Wales. Immediately he became passionate, the pencil was flung to the end of the room, the stool was kicked away and he was hardly able to apply himself at all. [Next day] he became very passionate because I told him he must not take out a walking stick in consequence of something crossing him when dressing. Later in the day he became violently angry because I wanted some Latin done; he flung things about, made grimaces, called me names and could not do anything for a long time.

Ten days after this, according to Gibbs, the tension in the school-room had increased:

A very bad day, the Prince of Wales has been like a person half silly. I could not gain his attention. He was very rude, particularly in the afternoon, throwing stones in my face. During his lesson in the morning he was running first in one place then in another. He made faces and spat. Dr Becker also complained of his great naughtiness. There was a great deal of bad words.

Within a few weeks Alfred began to share his brother's lessons, but he started to imitate Bertie's rudeness and disobedience. Mrs Anderson the music mistress complained to Gibbs that she could do nothing with either boy. Mr Leitch the drawing master did the same, but also revealed that Alfred was bullied by his elder brother who pulled his hair and kicked him if he felt like it, menacing him with a paper knife, while Mr Wellesley who gave them religious instruction said that both boys were inattentive and rude.

When out walking with the two boys Gibbs tried to enter into their play. Very naturally these games were all about brigands and fighting, and the tutor noticed how Bertie invariably demanded the chief role and always revelled in the violence. It was this which made Gibbs realise what Stockmar had meant when he warned him that this was 'a very difficult case, and requires the exercise of intellectual labour and thought'.

The Queen was very worried. In one of the talks she had with him, Gibbs wrote in his diary, she asked him if he thought that Bertie had been injured by being so much with the Princess Royal 'who is very clever and a child far above her age. She puts him down by a look—or a word—and their natural affection has been, she feared, impaired by this state of things.' Gibbs thought there might be some truth in this, for he had become more difficult since sharing his lessons with a younger and cleverer brother. Albert was soon forced to the conclusion that allowing the two boys to be taught together was not a good idea; the effect was the very opposite of what he intended, and instead of benefiting from the companionship and competition Alfred was becoming more unruly and slack every day. Gibbs' diary bears this out. 'His [Alfred's] attention has been distracted and when I called him back to his seat he refused to come. I spoke as kindly as possible—remonstrated, pointed out the folly and naughtiness of giving way to disobedience and temper—in vain.'

Frederick Gibbs would not have stayed as long as he did if it had not been for the companionship and support of Stockmar, who acted in his accustomed role of go-between with the Queen and

Albert, making them very well aware of the difficulties. The Queen enjoyed Mr Gibbs' company too, despite her assertion that she could not get on with learned men. Yet Frederick Weymouth Gibbs failed as lamentably as Henry Birch had done; he had made no progress at all with Bertie, and had to admit to the Queen that he could think of no way of getting the boy interested in intellectual matters. Besides, it was too difficult to teach a boy who could not stand criticism of any kind. In 1858 he too had gone.

'Poor Bertie,' the Queen wrote to Vicky, newly arrived in Prussia, 'he vexes us very much. There is not a particle of reflection or even attention to anything but dress. Not the slightest desire to learn, on the contrary, *il se bouche les oreilles* the moment anything of interest is being talked of!'

The burden now fell on General Bruce, brother of the charming Lady Augusta Bruce who was lady-in-waiting to the duchess of Kent and later on to the Queen. To lessen the load Albert himself took over some of the teaching as he had done with Vicky and was now doing with Alice, but without the same happy results. Bertie could not spit or make faces at his father, but he tried other equally annoying tactics; he was lazy and idle, fidgeted endlessly and answered 'yes, yes, yes', when he could not understand a word. It was hardly conduct to earn praise. Although irritated beyond endurance, Albert made efforts to keep his temper and tried to remember that one day Bertie would be king; he must not give up, otherwise what would happen to the throne? So he persevered, but his letters to Vicky about this time contain a note of bitterness and disappointment that he could not hide. If only the boy 'showed willing' sometimes, if only he tried, if only he could be interested in something. He took an almost perverse pleasure in being stupid, for Albert had noticed (and so had Lady Lyttelton some years before) that there were occasions when he could be quite sharp if it suited him.

His parents were hopeful again at Bertie's confirmation, when he was quiet and gentle and seemed properly impressed. The

Queen readily admitted that dressed in the Windsor uniform he made an engagingly slight figure as he stood before the Archbishop to be catechised.

Good behaviour brought its reward. He was gazetted a colonel (unattached) in the army for his seventeenth birthday and allowed to wear a uniform 'which he was as eager about as Arthur would have been at a bearskin and sword'. As an extra bonus he was to have a holiday in Berlin with Vicky, who had been longing for this for some time, and had made much of the good influence her brand-new husband would have on the wayward Bertie. The visit was a huge success. Bertie threw himself with gusto into a round of pleasures that left Vicky (expecting her first child) gasping. Fritz, on whose shoulders the responsibility for the boy's safety and good conduct fell, was driven half out of his wits chasing Bertie here, there and everywhere when he was not trying to prevent his licentious uncles taking the (willing) Bertie off to the hunting lodge in the hills for a 'bit of sport'.

By 1859 Victoria and Albert with great good sense decided that all they could ever hope to do with a character so full of anomalies was to bring out the boy's 'good kind qualities'. But as the months passed it became more and more difficult to keep their hopes alive, and in low moments the Queen moaned 'Oh what would happen if I were to die next winter!!' In view of the Prince of Wales's future conduct there was some reason for her anxiety. Rudyard Kipling was not so far off the mark when he called Victoria's heir 'a corpulent voluptuary of no importance', nor was Max Beerbohm too unkind when he drew a series of revealing cartoons that showed the Prince to be a most contemptible fellow. Albert never lived to see these nor many other marks of public derision which would have cut him to the quick.

Doggedly the work went on. In order to awaken a spark of enthusiasm for something, Albert decided to give his son a taste of the pleasures that he himself had enjoyed at the same age: walking tours in England and Switzerland, a trip to his Uncle

Ernest in Coburg, another to Italy where he had an audience of the
Pope as his father had done before him. Albert had a sneaking hope
that the glories of the art treasures would awaken some emotion in
the boy; if they did, the holidays would have been worthwhile. It
was all meant kindly and if Bertie returned with a mind a little
improved, so much the better.

Now that he was almost eighteen, Bertie was asserting his
personality by dressing in the latest fashion. To the Queen's dismay
he had his hair cut short, and Winterhalter had to paint him 'wearing a coiffure' that she thought 'really too hideous'. Moreover, his
hair plastered down to his head emphasised the Coburg nose which
she so detested: 'it makes him appear to be all head and no face',
she wailed to Vicky in despair. To give Bertie his due he was only
following the normal custom adopted by other young men of his
age. The Queen forgot that the wild Byronic curls of her youth
were fast disappearing and Bertie would have looked ridiculous if
he had not followed the latest trend. If only he had tried a little
harder to please them his parents would have treated his obsession
with clothes and fashion more leniently. They could have forgiven
a great deal if he had shown that he tried, if he had evinced an
interest in anything but smoking on the sly and enjoying himself
in society.

Unlike the other children he was not in the least musical, nor
did he care for drawing or reading. Pictures and sculpture left him
cold, which was a pity since it might have helped to draw father
and son together. Like the other members of the family he was
painted as a youth by Ross, Winterhalter and Landseer, but unlike
them he had not a scrap of interest in the way the painter produced
his colours and managed to catch a likeness. This lack of interest in
the arts was particularly distressing to Albert, under whose guidance the royal collection was now increasing fast. He and the
Queen not only bought old masters but as many modern paintings
as they could afford as well. They felt it their duty to patronise
living artists, especially those in need of money, so that others
might follow their example. They believed that art had to be

fostered carefully if it was to survive, and feared that in the next reign royal patronage of the arts would cease altogether. It was very sad that the one son who had inherited his father's interest and knowledge of art was Leopold, only six years old at the time of Albert's death.

Plans had been made to educate 'the nation's child' at Edinburgh, Oxford and Cambridge, and it was a relief to see him off to Scotland to begin his university career. Flattered to have the heir to the throne to teach, the Scottish dons saw talents in the boy which his parents never knew existed. Victoria and Albert were amazed but content to let things be. Oxford and Cambridge followed in turn and there is ample evidence that Bertie enjoyed himself enormously at both, despite a lot of nonsense which has been written to the contrary. He quickly realised that the minimum of work would satisfy the authorities. Away from the family, overshadowed by no one, he was for the first time Albert Edward, Prince of Wales, the future king of a powerful country.

He soon became the centre of attention, an attraction whenever he appeared: debonair and dressed in the latest fashion, he drew crowds like a magnet, much to his parents' annoyance. The dons much enjoyed the reflected glory that the prince's presence brought them and invited him frequently to dine at High Table, where his every word was listened to with grave attention. To his surprise Bertie learned what 'good chaps' dons could be. The undergraduates could not stand him at any price.

In the long vacation of 1860 Bertie was sent to Canada to open the railway bridge over the St Lawrence river at Montreal. Afterwards he travelled to Ottawa to lay the foundation stone of the Federal Parliament building. The trip was a huge success from start to finish. Here at last was something he enjoyed doing and for which he showed enthusiasm—to be exhibited to thousands of people, to bow and wave to crowds whose cheers deafened his ears, were pleasures that never palled. It came as a pleasant shock to his parents to be told that the tour was such a triumph. Fêted wherever he went, this most autocratic of young men was hailed as a 'truly democratic Prince'. At last he had found his vocation; his father aptly named him 'ambassador extraordinary'.

Albert did not live long enough to see his son married to the lovely Princess Alexandra of Denmark, but it was a match that had his blessing. Had he lived, Alexandra's married life, so filled with unhappiness and humiliation, might have run an easier course.

3

Alice

'Life was made for work and not pleasure'

ANOTHER DAUGHTER WAS born to Victoria and Albert on 25 April 1843 and given the names Alice Maud Mary. This time the arrival of a girl did not give Albert even a momentary feeling of disappointment, for Vicky's companionable nature and her admiration of her father had shown him the advantages of daughters over sons. Not only were they less trouble, but he innocently believed a remark his grandmother Augusta had once made—that sons left the parental roof as quickly as they could but that daughters remained at home to be a solace to their parents in old age.

Confronted with the real thing (so different from what they imagined) Victoria and Albert found the longwinded and complicated memoranda they had written while awaiting the arrival of their first child now seemed very out-of-date, even absurd. The young parents were learning how different each baby could be and that when in doubt it was simpler to rely on trial and error rather than some hard and fast rule laid down beforehand. Three years later, with a well-run nursery and Lady Lyttelton (a woman who had learned by experience with her own children) at hand to consult, everything seemed easy and relaxed. Albert too was taking his parental duties more lightly; when he ran into the nursery, he did so cheerfully and not with an anxiously beating heart, expecting to find something wrong.

Since 1840 a few more taboos had gone out of the window; Stockmar had ordered caps to be discarded in the nursery—it was nonsense that the open fontanelle needed to be protected in this way. Nor was the baby's face to be covered by a veil any more when the child took an airing in the arms of Mrs Lilly the stout monthly nurse. There was to be no more superstitious nonsense in this modern nursery, so baby Alice was not 'carried upstairs before she went down'; in consequence Stockmar was very unpopular with Mrs Lilly, who was of the old school. The fuss and anxiety that went on when Vicky was vaccinated was also a thing of the past. Victoria and Albert now took such precautions as a matter of course; Albert no longer felt it necessary to be present, as he had with Vicky and Bertie, looking so tense and worried that the children were screaming before they were touched. It was taken for granted that when Alice was three months old Mr Brown the Windsor apothecary would come to the Castle to vaccinate her (as was the custom then he took the vaccine from the arm of another baby). Fortunately all the children proved good subjects for Edward Jenner's lifesaving discovery. The royal family were always among the first to support any advance in medicinal knowledge which had been tested and proved reasonably safe, feeling it their duty to show the way. Queen Victoria had chloroform for the birth of her eighth child in 1854, before it came into common use, and found its effects remarkably soothing and helpful.

But on one point she remained adamant; she would not feed the child herself. So there was another hunt by Dr Clark for a healthy wet nurse, who was eventually found in the wilds of Wales and brought to Buckingham Palace. The nurse was warned straight away that there was to be no self-indulgence with food. Stockmar put her on to a strict diet of boiled mutton, supplemented between meals by bowls of bread and milk and beef tea, so that she put on weight faster than the baby. As a precaution the key of the medicine cupboard remained on Stockmar's key ring so that no unauthorised laudanum or silver nitrate could be slipped into the child's teething powders in order to give the nurses a peaceful night.

Although not a beauty, from all accounts Alice was a merry little thing, very fat and contented, but with her fair share of that rumbustious temperament that so often got her elder sister Vicky into hot water. The fact that she cried less than the other two was

The Prince of Wales in a sailor suit by Winterhalter

Princess Alice by Winterhalter

put down to her easy birth, for Queen Victoria suffered very little this time and her recovery was rapid. There was no post-natal depression to cause tears and exhaustion, no irritability and touchiness that had made her so difficult to deal with last time. The auguries for a long and happy life for Alice seemed good, but in fact this child was to become the most complex of all the Queen's children and to die at the early age of thirty-five.

Although Victoria and Albert considered royal christenings should be private affairs, Albert could not resist the temptation to use them to cement political alliances that might benefit England. But Queen Victoria preferred family sponsors for this child, taking the sensible view that great connections were all very well for a Princess Royal or a Prince of Wales, who could be expected to make important dynastic marriages, but that for the more insignificant younger children relations would be of more use. Their choice for Alice was bizarre, to say the least. The Queen saw nothing incongruous in inviting the King of Hanover (her uncle Ernest of Cumberland who had been so rude to Albert) despite his murky past, and Albert's brother Ernest, whose licentious habits had made them both curse him for 'dragging the Coburg name in the mud'. Despite the close blood connection, neither of her sponsors had one spark of tender feeling for the child, nor did they respond some years later to her pleas for help during troubled times in Darmstadt.

Life for the royal children was very free and no one benefited more from this than Alice, whose nature required few restrictions. It was as though she had been born with a ready-made capacity for self-discipline which occasionally could be pure masochism. She was not shy, but she had a remarkable ability (since she was one of a large noisy family) to keep her feelings to herself, and although as a child she was seldom seen without a smile on her face this gave little indication of what was going on inside her head. Later on the battles of life stamped a mournful look on her face, as every painting and photograph shows. Stockmar, who missed nothing, was quick to sense that Alice was not very capable of fending for herself. If Bertie snatched her toys from her, it was Vicky who flew at him and got them back. Whenever battles raged in the nursery or schoolroom, Alice would withdraw into her shell until they were over, for she was always afflicted by doubt over the cause of the fight—who was in the right and who in the wrong? In that way she was the very opposite of Vicky, who knew no such hesitations but took on all comers if her temper was roused without stopping to think. But Alice was clever enough to recognise her lack of confidence as a fault which she must conquer if she was to succeed in life; the trouble was that she never quite managed this and often felt low in consequence. It was an irony of fate that the one child of Victoria and Albert who most needed protection and security in order to achieve happiness was to have to live without both from the day she left home as a married woman.

In her early years there were few signs that this lively little girl was to become an introverted young woman. We read of her running in and out of Stockmar's room with the others, scrambling on to his knees, joining in her brothers' rough play, talking unselfconsciously with strangers, winning the King of Saxony's lasting affection by unselfishly offering to share her last piece of bread-and-butter with him.

Like most children Alice could never describe which of her holiday homes made her happiest. At 'dear Osborne' she forgot that anywhere else existed, but a month or two later 'dear Balmoral' was the most blessed place in the world, there was nothing like it. Her feelings for both were very intense: she dried flowers from their gardens and pressed them in a book to remind her of happy times. Houses that she was familiar with meant a great deal to Alice; to leave one for another was a frequent cause of tears. Years later, with children of her own, she deplored her parents' habit of moving from Windsor to Osborne then perhaps to Balmoral or Buckingham Palace so frequently that no sooner had they settled down in one place than they were whisked off to another. In her case, it was an ordeal that she found hard to face and she began to dread each move even before it had begun.

Because she was ashamed of these feelings and knew that they were not shared by the others, she never confided in her father but hugged them so closely to herself that they did much to bring on the depressions which bewildered and upset her. For the first week or two at Balmoral, however, she revelled in the lack of restriction which allowed her to run about alone, visiting the cottagers without ceremony, happy that she was indistinguishable from other children in her kilt—kilts were handed down from child to child irrespective of sex. She loved her pony, yet paradoxically rode the animal into the hills without due care, risking a scolding from the Queen who never allowed her ponies to be overworked. All her life she remembered with pleasure these all-day excursions into the hills, a huge cavalcade of family and servants loaded down with picnic-baskets, sketch-books and rugs. Landseer recorded many of these picnics against a background of mountain and heather. Albert looks strangely unlike himself in deerstalker and check coat, so does Queen Victoria wrapped up against the wind in her plaid. Only the children look themselves, busy in their own pursuits.

Although she was reluctant to admit it (for she was always putting up defences to prevent herself from being hurt) Alice was happier at Osborne than anywhere else. In the softer, milder climate of the Isle of Wight the pace was slower and less strenuous than in Scotland. Life at the seaside appealed to her more too because of her passion for swimming and the opportunities which playing on the sands presented to her imagination. Alice was the only one of the children to suffer seriously from the cold and like her father she needed continual exercise to keep her circulation going. Osborne gave her the warmth so necessary for her well-being; there, even in the sharpest spring weather her fingers were not covered with chilblains, there was no painful cramp in her toes, her nose was never red nor her lips blue with cold. More important still was the feeling of safety and seclusion the island gave her; away from the roar of the outside world, the disasters that she imagined might strike them all faded into nothing, leaving her relaxed and peaceful. Something in Osborne too brought out the curious mixture of qualities in Alice's nature. The dreamer in her fed on solitary walks in the woods with their dark and threatening corners, on poetry (especially Tennyson) and on the romantic novels which she read in the shade of a tree when it was too hot to play. Her practical side found an outlet in the domesticity of the Swiss cottage, where she would enthusiastically bake cakes for a family tea, or in vigorous work in her own small garden in the grounds. But gardening did not have the same happy results with her as with Vicky and Alfred, for her father's horticultural genius had passed her by.

This original and imaginative holiday home left an indelible mark on the growing Alice; long periods in its peaceful, undemanding atmosphere gave her time to think about herself and get to grips with her own nature in her own way. Because few outsiders were invited to Osborne, Alice's great capacity for affection found an outlet in riding with her father, reading with her mother and the companionship of her brothers and sisters. Without thinking much about it, she came to understand that everything they did together revolved round the real head of the house—her father, who created all their pleasures, all their fun. Whatever happened in the day, the evenings at Osborne were the times when they were closest as a family. There would be music, reading aloud from a book chosen to suit young and old alike, or a crazy card game invented on the spur of the moment by Albert, so that they all went happy and laughing to bed. It is sad to think that in later years as a married woman there were periods when she was so at odds with her widowed mother that she received no invitation to Osborne in the summer. Deeply wounded, she took her children to Blankenburghe or Eastbourne; but she could never recreate the atmosphere of her own happy childhood in either.

If Bertie's intellect was often compared disadvantageously to Vicky's, no one ever thought of doing the same with Alice, although she was not as clever as her sister. This mild treatment may have been because she was such a reasonable child that she never irritated anyone's nerves by showing stubbornness or impertinently answering back. Lady Lyttelton and the under-governesses would explain things to her patiently because she so much wanted to do her best. It was only when she entered her teens that she began to show the intellectual promise that made her such an interesting woman later on. As a child she uttered none of those lightning flashes of wit which made Vicky so amusing at the same age, and there are no stories of her droll remarks. But she was observant and missed little; she could recall with a wealth of detail events which had happened years before and which everyone else had forgotten. The impression that she gave was of a pleasant competent young girl, obedient and with a quiet charm that made her much liked. 'Good amiable Alice', was Queen Victoria's understated praise for so worthy a daughter. Beneath the surface, however, a great deal more lay hidden, though only Vicky sensed the tendency to needless self-sacrifice, the compulsion to martyrdom.

Vicky and Alice were devoted to each other; they shared a bedroom and all their secret hopes and fears, borrowed each other's clothes as sisters always do, and together they formed an alliance against the rest of the world. All through her life Alice found a spirited defender in Vicky, whose dearest wish was to have Alice marry a member of the Prussian royal family so that they would still be close together even though married. Yet despite this love between them Alice could not help but suffer in comparison with Vicky's greater talents. It was no fun for her to live in the shadow of a sister who was not only a strong personality but an irresistibly charming one as well. She did not feel jealousy or envy, only a burning desire to be other than she was—in other words, much more like Vicky.

Alice had many talents of her own that she did not rate highly enough. She was beautiful dancer, a graceful skater, an accomplished horsewoman, the only one of the sisters with a real flair for clothes. Her first sight of a crinoline—worn by the Empress Eugénie at Windsor in April 1855—was a revelation; in a flash she recognised the magical effect of simplicity in an age of frills and flounces. She loved music and played the piano well, drew competently and had a gift for acting. Miss Hildyard, who stage-managed their plays and *tableaux vivants*, gave her the most difficult parts as a matter of course.

More than the others, Alice was deeply conscious of her position as a member of a ruling family—not that she wanted to demand homage but because she had to make herself face up to her responsibilities. This sometimes meant that she demanded too high a standard from herself, but it did not make her rigid, for she was addicted to 'pranks and larks' even at the expense of rank and dignity, and the household always turned a blind eye when she slipped into St George's Chapel in ordinary clothes and sat at the back rubbing shoulders with her mother's subjects. It was innocent enough fun and the natural result of having young parents and unconventional holidays, but it gave her a feeling of escape which was important to her. Lord Clarendon's daughter Constance wrote that she was 'just like a bird in a cage beating its wings against the bars and if she could get out wouldn't she go it?' This is what Alice herself believed. It was only as she grew older that she began to realise that the barriers she imagined round her were not those of rank but consisted of more mundane things like lack of purpose and appreciation, intellectual barrenness and poverty. Sadly, she was to labour in a soil that was unreceptive of the seed she tried to sow.

Somewhere in her formative years she began to lack confidence seriously and to develop a feeling of inferiority, although in 1858 she took Vicky's place as her father's favourite pupil. Her wounds were often self-inflicted because even this did not convince her that she was clever enough to please her father or good enough to please her mother. Queen Victoria slapped down her shortcomings with a heavy hand, as she did with all the children, but the effect on Alice was quite the opposite to what she intended—it depressed her instead of leading to improvement since she lacked Vicky's ability to laugh at herself.

After Alice's confirmation in 1859 the Queen forgot all about her good resolution to allow her to stay at home for a year or two as the daughter of the house. Albert had begged Victoria not to bother about finding a husband for a few years, but the Queen refused to listen and began to fidget—as though a girl could be left on the shelf at seventeen. She made it very evident that she put little faith in Alice's looks, but this was simply because her long nose, pale skin and straight hair did not correspond to the current idea of beauty. (In fact, she was the image of her great-grand-mother Augusta, who had a face of character and distinction.) It was impossible for Queen Victoria to keep her fears to herself, so that Alice began to believe that she really was too plain to marry. Albert caught the habit of referring to her as 'poor dear Alice' or 'good Alice' (he had never called Vicky anything like that) although there is abundant evidence that he thought highly of her. In one way Alice looked forward to marriage, believing that it would give her more opportunities to do all that she wanted to do in life. But her inferiority complex was not improved by having her future mismanaged. Early in 1859 the Queen thought that she had found just the right husband for her second daughter in the Prince of Orange and invited him to Buckingham Palace for inspection. He came and saw but did not conquer; he was rude to Alice at a dinner party and 'that settled her feelings about him'. Eventually she picked on Louis of Hesse-Darmstadt, heir presumptive to the dukedom, a kindly but not very clever young man, who had seen little of the world. Louis was slow to come to the point, much to Alice's shame, and had to be given an ultimatum some-what roughly by Albert, who must take his share of the blame in not realising Louis's limitations. Albert saw in Louis talents and aspirations he could not possibly possess and managed to delude himself into believing that Alice's prospective husband was almost his equal. Very naturally Alice took him at her father's valuation and fell deeply in love, not understanding how much her parents were swayed by the fact that Louis was an 'innocent' young man who had not indulged in illicit affairs.

No blame attaches to Queen Victoria for her lack of insight into the complexities of Alice's character. Nine children and her duties as Queen kept her busy, and it is remarkable by any standards that she managed to do so much. It was not that she was blind to Alice's virtues, only that as a woman of her time she thought it wrong to overpraise them; her mistake, if it can be called that, was to treat all her children alike. That she had no idea of what went on in Alice's mind is clear from a letter she wrote to Vicky in 1858:

> Your saying you thought a young girl not in an enviable position comes a little I think from that proud high spirit, which you will remember we did all we could to check and which it would have been so wrong in us to have tolerated. I am sure you feel now, my dear child, how right and wise we were. But you were trying. Alice I don't think feels a young girl's life trying —she is really very good, so amiable, so gentle, so obliging and so humble.

Preparing for her marriage was a happy time for Alice. Although she had less of a scientific bent than Vicky, medicine had always interested her enormously and after her engagement she was at pains to read medical books so that she might be able to understand the process of childbirth and treat minor illnesses at home. Yet this newly acquired knowledge could not help her in her father's last illness. All it did was to destroy her peace of mind, because it showed her how desperately ill he was and how badly he was being nursed. During those terrible weeks, Alice showed a strength of character that amazed all who knew her. She put aside all thoughts of self as she encouraged her mother and played or sang to her father, showing a serene face that hid a heart weighed down with anxiety and fear. When the blow fell, it was Alice who became her widowed mother's main support, shutting herself up alone with her for weeks on end at Osborne, sharing the strain with no one. Albert's death could not have happened at a worse time for her. If she was not to waste her talents, she still needed her father's guiding hand even in the first years of marriage, since her husband was not her intellectual equal. Albert would have given her the confidence she so sadly lacked and had he lived she might never have called her life 'rather a disappointing one'. Only in the friendships of her later life did she follow the lines Albert would have marked out: Florence Nightingale, Octavia Hill, Ruskin and Carlyle encouraged her interest in improving the lot of women, and in Darmstadt she sought the company of David Strauss, the ageing philosopher and theologian who to some extent filled the gap left by the father she missed so much.

4

Alfred

'He is a good, dear, clever, odd boy'

VICTORIA AND ALBERT'S fourth child was the son destined before
he was born on 6 August 1844 to be duke of Saxe-Coburg-Gotha.
Albert's brother Ernest was childless and it was beginning to look
as though he would always remain so. In order to secure the
succession he made Albert promise that once there was a Prince of
Wales, the next boy would be his heir. From every point of view
it was a good arrangement, but Albert, knowing his brother very
well, laid down conditions. It was important, he insisted, to remember that if Bertie died young, Alfred would automatically
succeed to the British throne, so that he must be educated for both
rôles, the lesser one necessarily taking second place. Ernest had to
be content with this, but he never ceased trying to get the boy into
his clutches, wanting to keep him for long periods in Coburg and
treating him as his own child. Lest this should mean—as Albert
feared it might—that Alfred would be initiated into his uncle's
debauched ways, Albert tried to keep Ernest's bad influence to the
minimum by never allowing the boy to stay for more than short
periods in Coburg.

From the start Affie (as he was soon called) was a most satisfactory child, alert but contented, seldom bad-tempered and on good
terms with everyone. In looks he was every inch a Coburger, with
none of his father's fairness; he had dark hair, very deep blue eyes,
a prominent nose (Queen Victoria was thankful that he had not
inherited the true thick Coburg nose) and skin not as white as that
of the other children. As he grew up he became if anything more
cheerful, self-contained and versatile, quite content to be alone but
equally happy to be one of a boisterous group of children. He took

what came with philosophic calm, meeting every vicissitude in the same cool way. For balance and reliability he could not be beaten and yet Albert saw that he had other qualities that must be harnessed and controlled if they were to be of use to him. As soon as he could walk alone, Affie made it very evident that he was utterly fearless, even foolhardy. Danger did not exist for him, and his recklessness soon became the bane of his parents' and his nurses' lives. Victoria and Albert never knew what the boy would be up to next, and on more than one occasion they returned home to find that he had only just escaped breaking his neck. Unless continually watched he would climb out of windows and balance on ledges over a thirty- or forty-foot drop, leap across deep fast-running streams before he could swim, or sneak into a field to ride bareback on the wildest ponies. When still very young he slid down the banisters at Balmoral, fell headlong on to the stone floor and almost cracked his skull. Though severely scolded, he did the same thing again next day with the same result. Hardly a week passed without Affie having some accident, but he never broke a limb, so that his parents began to hope that he led a charmed life. Scoldings, whippings, a period of solitary confinement, all had no effect. What was to be done with such a boy?

Nevertheless, he was a favourite with everyone, winning Lady Lyttelton's heart by his good temper, honesty, aptitude for learning and willingness to share his toys. He showed all the concentration Bertie lacked and brought harmony to the nursery at a time when his elder brother was becoming difficult to handle. 'Prince Alfred continues highly intelligent and very attractive', she wrote to her daughter when he was nearly four. 'He does little new except a little geography and that he remembers from day to day strangely, but he begins to read so as to understand at once and his dear calm penetrating blue eyes are so expressive he must turn out well.'

This interest in geography went hand in hand with his passion for the sea and for ships. From a very early age there was not a vessel in the Queen's Navy that he could not name and describe down to the smallest detail. Whenever he was given a drawing lesson, he was unwilling to sketch anything but ships and sea battles. Where the sea was concerned his imagination knew no bounds. His bedroom looked as much like a cabin as he could make it, with a ship's clock and a barometer which his father had given him one birthday. Curiosity to find out for himself more about ships and the men who manned them and the places they sailed to spurred Affie on to read early. One of his happiest playgrounds quickly became Stockmar's room with its two large terrestrial and celestial globes standing between the windows. The Baron would draw up a stool for the little boy to stand on, seating himself in a chair close by, and when all was ready the interrogation would begin. What is this country called? How far away is it from us? How old must I be before I can go there?

Next to ships Affie's passion was for animals, especially dogs. Like Queen Victoria, he never moved without his pets who slept on his bed and on all the sofas and chairs; he was usually to be seen exercising what seemed dozens of dogs whenever he took a walk in the grounds. He taught them tricks in order to surprise and amaze his parents, so delighting his mother that she boasted that if he were not her son he might earn a living with his troupe in a travelling circus.

There was an industrious streak in this boy sadly lacking in the heir to the throne. He was never idle, but always busy and happily employed on some project of his own. He never said he was bored, asked what he should do next or expected to be amused. It was impossible, as the Queen said, not to see the contrast 'with someone who shall be nameless'. Frequently his parents would come across Affie deeply absorbed in what he was doing, unaware of his surroundings or that anyone was watching him. One of the things he liked to do was to take mechanical objects to pieces in order to remake them with improvements or to invent some strange mechanical toy to amuse the younger children, and he would spend hours hammering and sawing bits of wood, tin and leather until he got just what he wanted. Once he managed to make a musical box that squeaked out what the others declared to be 'Rule Britannia'. What did it matter that it only worked by fits and starts? It was an achievement and Affie was praised for it.

Each day was filled with interest and excitement for this highly imaginative child, and the results of his labours kept his brothers and sisters enraptured; even watching him at work was a delight in itself, for they never knew what he would do next. The little girls in particular found him good-tempered and willing to help them do things they found difficult, so that he was much in demand at the Swiss cottage for stoking the stove, carrying water, mending broken cups and saucers, even peeling potatoes and shelling peas. His labours done, he would go off whistling to the carpenter's shop, to continue working on his latest model ship. 'He is full of cheerfulness', Albert wrote to Ernest, reporting progress in 1857, 'I hope that this will stay with him throughout his life'.

Affie's predilection for the sea made Osborne a paradise. He swam like a fish, was always eager to be off in the little *Fairy* (whose engine he often tinkered with far more effectively than his father) on those 'marine excursions' Queen Victoria so much enjoyed. Nothing could have suited Affie better than to be at sea in a storm when the order to abandon ship was given, for he was always asking for permission to test the lifeboats. But when he witnessed a collision at sea from the deck of the royal yacht he was more shaken than he expected, though not daunted. Young though he was he kept his head and helped his father and the men fling the lifebelts into the sea to save the lives of those who could not swim.

Affie admired his elder brother and was the only one of the children who, by drawing Bertie into his games, could calm his rages and curtail his bullying, because the games kept him occupied and so counteracted the boredom and the inability to make his own amusements which were the main causes of Bertie's extraordinary behaviour. The experiment of teaching the boys together was an attempt to capitalise on this but (as has been remarked already) was a dismal failure because admiration made Alfred copy all Bertie's bad ways. Poor Gibbs found himself with two rude and inattentive pupils to cope with instead of one. So the brothers were parted again, entirely for Affie's good—but posterity has not hesitated to make the error of calling this a senseless violation of Bertie's affections by his cruel father.

At this stage Affie was no more bookish than Bertie. Except for sea stories, reading for its own sake did not interest him much. But his parents did not hold this against him, because he had proved that he could be persevering and painstaking and shown that he always used his talents to the full. It was important to Albert that his spontaneity and his high principles should be fostered and developed so that when the time came to take on the duties of ruling Coburg, he would be able rapidly to repair the damage which Ernest's profligacy and extravagance had caused. 'High principles, moral fibre and a liberal attitude, with constant watchfulness and industry', he said, were the very qualities needed to ensure this. It had been apparent at Affie's confirmation that his heart could be touched when he broke down and wept in the middle of the Archbishop's address.

Albert often made time to talk to Affie about Coburg and Thuringia, stressing their importance because the ducal family now occupied so many European thrones. Previous dukes, he told Affie, had been remarkable not for imposing high taxes and ignoring their subjects' welfare (like his brother Ernest at the present moment) but by unselfishness and devotion to duty. The example to follow was that of his grandmother the duchess Augusta, who was adored in her lifetime and still remembered. These talks with Affie so carried Albert away that he had to remind himself sharply that the boy might never be duke of Coburg but king of England instead.

Although it was thus doubly necessary for Affie to be well educated, there was no 'plan' quite as explicit as that drawn up for Bertie. Father and son understood each other very well, however, so that a year or two before Albert would have begun his evening lessons, Affie took the initiative of asking his father to teach him as he had taught Vicky. The lessons were a great success. Affie showed powers of concentration and an eagerness which, although less remarkable than his sister's, made him a pleasure to teach; it partly compensated for the irritation Albert had to suffer when Bertie's attention wandered during a lesson.

Periodical reports of Affie's progress went to Ernest in Coburg. Albert was as regular about sending them as he was resolute about not handing the boy over to his brother's care. A letter he wrote to Ernest in 1857 also shows how well he understood his son:

> First, as regards his wish to enter the navy; this is a *passion* which we, as his parents, believe we have no right to oppose, because it never does any good to withstand the spontaneous desires of youthful spirit. We have done what we can not to encourage it, and since it goes along with a strong inclination for science, particularly mechanics, we have assigned a young engineer officer to him, hoping that he will be able to interest him in this branch of the service. But his love for the blue jacket has always shown through and, given the remarkable perseverance of the child, it is not to be expected that he will give the idea up. An example of his perseverance is his violin, which he learned to play secretly, in his spare time, as a surprise for us; he cannot be parted from it. Another example is his mechanical models, to which he devotes every spare moment. On the other hand, we should have to consider what he would do if he were not allowed to enter the navy. We two are 37 and 36 years old, and therefore have the right to expect that we may live another 20 or 25 years. What is Affie to do in these 25 years? If he enters the navy he will have enjoyed all there is to enjoy in that time. The service will make him acquainted with all parts of the world and he will have become more generally capable than he would by staying here or in Germany. The service, with its strict discipline and the early responsibility it gives young officers, is a marvellous training for life.

It had been necessary to write to Ernest at some length because he had lately been pressing very hard again to have Affie with him permanently. The years were passing, he said, and the boy was already almost fourteen; it was high time for him to live in Coburg for a period to develop his German side. Politely and laboriously Albert explained all over again that only 'two eyes' stood between Alfred and the British throne. If he were to become king of England, what chance of success would he have if he had been educated almost entirely abroad and knew nothing of the way his subjects thought and felt? He met Ernest's peevish complaint that since Coburg was landlocked, a naval career would be of no use to its duke, with the frank admission that Alfred's passion for the sea meant that there was a real risk of the navy creating in him a distaste for life in a small German state; 'the danger is there', he told Ernest, 'and we must meet it as best we can'. However, Albert realised that at this stage some concessions would have to be made:

We have to bear in mind the possibility that he might come to the throne here—and that if we have made a German out of him we shall have given him a great deal to live down, while on the other hand it could be a positive advantage to come from greater matters to the lesser affairs of Coburg. Since boys enter the navy at 14 or 15, we had 18 months to play with. It seemed desirable that he should get to know the Continent, and particularly to speak French. That, and the ease of getting a good teacher, made us decide for Geneva. But there are also two other considerations—first that the small German courts are not unjustifiably accused of illiberality here, and my connection with them is always held against me, so that the experiment of sending one of our sons to be educated at one of them would have met with the greatest opposition and have the worst construction put upon it in the public mind. There is actually something attractive to the English in the experiment itself. The choice of republican Switzerland and traditionally Protestant Geneva has been received well, granted that an experiment of this kind was to be made at all. Now the time is coming when he has to prepare himself for the navy. To fulfil your natural wish to have Alfred with you, and so that he shall get to know his German homeland while he is still young, he shall come back via Coburg and Gotha. He will not have much time, but could spend a week in each place. He has to leave Geneva about 1 May and to meet us at Osborne for Victoria's birthday or a day or two beforehand. He will have three weeks for his journey, and two of these he could spend with you. Let me know if this suits you and if you will show him the two places. For the moment please keep this secret. Let me hear soon what you think.

Alfred joined the navy in 1858 at the age of fourteen. The Queen was in an agony at losing this amusing child who had such a good effect on the rest of the family, and Albert too was depressed at his going. The only one to show pleasure and excitement was the new naval cadet himself. 'All the arrangements for Affie's going to sea have been made', the Queen wrote dismally to Vicky, 'he will go on board the *Euryalus*, commanded by Captain Tarleton whom you saw at Osborne.' The break was made easier by Affie first entering the training school at Alverstoke near Gosport, a mere stone's throw from Osborne House, and so the Queen's next letter to Vicky is considerably more cheerful. She could see Affie as often as she liked, and indeed did see him more often than Affie's commanding officer bargained for. 'Affie is going on admirably', she wrote, 'he is coming to luncheon today which is a real brilliant Osborne day.'

Shouts of joy greeted his arrival; he had not changed a bit (he had only been away a week). After stuffing himself with cakes at the Swiss cottage, he was soon in the tool-shed covered in grease, showing off his homemade air pump and steam engine to his admiring family. Unfortunately they did not work quite as they should that day.

When his training was finished and he went to sea, Affie made up for his badly expressed and ill-spelt letters by retailing in detail during his brief leaves at home everything he had seen and done and everybody he had spoken to, so that his mother felt quite part of his life.

He was growing up fast, but still did not wash his hands properly. Instead of being irritated, the Queen rather enjoyed these signs that he was unsophisticated and still a child. Yet he had matured in one way; after a large dinner party at Buckingham Palace, the first he had ever attended as a fully fledged adult, he mingled easily with the guests and talked to everyone in a most natural and unselfconscious manner. 'Faults he still has', the Queen wrote in one of her daily letters to Prussia; but even these, never very glaring, were becoming less. Her pride in him was justified for he passed his examinations with high marks and was delighted when his parents showed their pleasure.

Like his elder brother before him Affie was allowed to spend a holiday with Vicky in Prussia, accompanied by the faithful Major Cowell, overwhelming Vicky with joy at having this adored young brother all to herself. They were like two puppies tearing along the corridors at Babelsberg, a palace that had never before echoed to the sound of young laughter. Every day was packed full of excitement, with riding and picnics and with exploring historic places Vicky had not yet seen, but most glorious of all spending lazy hours boating on the Haviel when they talked themselves hoarse and then rushed home before evening fell to play another round of that fascinating new game of croquet. Their frolics earned a sharp reproof from Queen Victoria who had hoped that in Vicky's company Affie would imbibe a little of the culture which was so lacking in the navy; but they both felt that it was worth it.

Albert died on 14 December 1861 while Affie was away at sea. His death marked the end of childhood. The shock and the agony of not knowing at a distance exactly what had happened hit Affie hard, and at sixteen he had to learn the cruel lesson that there is no place on a ship for private grief. After the first rush of tears his sorrow had to be hidden and shared with no one. The bond with his father which had been the most important factor in his life had been strengthened by their mutual interest in Coburg. During his first visit the year before, Alfred had discovered to his great delight that he was experiencing much the same feelings of peace and contentment at the Rosenau that his father had enjoyed many years before at the same age, and suddenly he was moved by the first stirrings of excitement at the thought that some time in the future the duchy would be his.

On his first leave after his father's death the change that had come over a once happy home distressed him deeply because he was too young to understand and sympathise with his mother's prostration; the air of grief and desolation that hung over everything dampened his spirits and alienated him from her. Nothing would ever make him forget his father and he felt aggrieved when accused of heartlessness if he laughed, whistled or played his violin. He would have returned to sea very forlorn had not his future sister-in-law Princess Alexandra of Denmark, who was much the same age and who came to Osborne to be inspected as Bertie's future wife a week before Affie went to sea again, done everything in her power to help him recover. She let him talk freely to her of his father and of his own happy childhood and all it meant to him when lonely and far away from home. There was more than a grain of truth in Queen Victoria's remark that if Bertie did not want Alix, Affie would marry her like a shot if she could wait until he was older.

The beginnings of a rift between the Queen and Alfred can be detected within a year or two of Albert's death, after Affie had blotted his copy-book by having an affair with a girl while his ship was stationed at Malta. Of course there were extenuating circumstances which the Queen in her grief and disappointment refused to listen to—the boredom of the place, the relaxed behaviour of the other naval officers, the countless opportunities coupled with not enough to do. But the Queen wanted her sons to be pure as the driven snow in order to be worthy of the dead father whom she was in the process of deifying. She used exaggerated terms to describe Alfred's fall from grace—'horrified'—'broken hearted'— 'quite bowed down with it'. Her shattered illusions made her 'weak and ill', so that she suffered 'bitter anguish'. All this was poured out to Vicky who replied with a sympathetic but sensible letter, hoping that her mother would see the affair in the right perspective:

> How could Affie be such a goose to play such a silly trick and stand in his own light. I feel so pained to think that he should have been so thoughtless as to add to your grief by his misbehaviour. I feel the dear boy is not yet so conscientious as he should be, but I hope dearest Mama you will not distress yourself too much about this.

This letter of Vicky's had the good effect of making Queen Victoria pause and look at the culprit properly. For the first time she saw that he was pale and woebegone, but the effect did not last long. Only a short while before, Affie had earned praise by not becoming dazzled by the offer of the throne of Greece, preferring to stand by the promise he had made to his father to take on the far from glittering prize of Coburg and the burden of his uncle Ernest's mountain of debts. High principles did not weigh with Queen Victoria unless they were accompanied by 'moral tone'. Unhappily there was no one to save the situation, no one but Vicky (and she was hundreds of miles away and could only communicate by letter) to tell Queen Victoria that this affair must not be magnified, that the sooner it was forgotten the better. Mother and son began to drift apart, slowly at first, almost imperceptibly, and in future the only moments of closeness were ephemeral. The Queen's anguish was genuine when in April 1863 she learned that he had contracted typhoid fever in Naples, and again in 1865 when a supporter of the Irish revolutionary Fenian brotherhood had shot him between the ribs while he was presiding at a public picnic in Australia. Affie's luck held on the second occasion and his life was saved by two nurses trained by Florence Nightingale who had recently arrived in Sydney infirmary. 'God has been very merciful in sparing him', the Queen wrote to Vicky, but added tartly, 'I trust for good'.

It was not unnatural that after a period at sea, Alfred should want to go out in society when on leave in London, but the Queen could not see this and was annoyed when he did so. Young, handsome and rich, he was much in demand, especially at the Marlborough House balls and receptions, where he partnered his sister-in-law in all the newest dances and made the Queen fear that he might still be more than half in love with the fascinating Alix. But it was Constance Grosvenor, the wife of the duke of Westminster, twelve years his senior, whom he fell 'violently in love with'. Evidently this unrequited passion did not improve his temper, for the Queen complained he had become hard and unsympathetic: 'so sharp and unkind in speaking to others when he disagrees, and he always knows best'.

Matters went from bad to worse. Thoroughly at odds with the world, at home Alfred became as violent as he dared (the House-hold groaned, fearing fireworks when he turned up at Balmoral), thankful when he came on leave less and less often. When he did deign to stay for a few days, he made it plain that he found court circles a bore and despised his mother for indulging herself in grief and making mourning an excuse to spoil the fun of others. Nor did he trouble to hide his loathing for the dour Scot, John Brown, on whom Queen Victoria depended increasingly, so that it was all Sir Henry Ponsonby (the Queen's private secretary) could do to keep the peace.

What had happened to the cheerful little boy whom everyone loved? Since his father's death Affie had been suffering first from the effects of shock and then from the pain of being left without guidance at so early an age. More than any of the children, Affie needed someone dependable to confide in because he was so often far from home, moving among strangers and continually facing new situations. Unfortunately in the early days of her bereavement the Queen was in no fit state to take over the father's place or to understand what was happening to this once happy boy, and soon it was too late.

Some years later there was a sudden change for the better when Affie fell seriously in love with the Grand Duchess Marie of Russia. The prospect of the union alarmed the Queen. She feared priests in and out of Marlborough House and the effect their presence would have on her people; but she never had reason to regret the marriage, although the Imperial family did turn a bit grand and refused the Queen's request that Marie should come and be looked over first. The slight was only allayed by Marie herself, who was unaffected, straightforward and loyal, showing a willingness to adopt many of the Queen's own ideas about how a royal princess should behave and winning her affection by going among the people 'in a very right and proper manner'. According to Queen Victoria, Marie was no beauty although she was healthy and had fine teeth and skin, but Vicky was possibly nearer the truth when she said that Marie's looks were of a kind that 'grew on one'. She possessed one asset that was prized by the family beyond jewels: she was not in the least intimidated by her formidable mother-in-law, with whom she could quite hold her own.

The marriage took place on 23 January 1873 in the chapel of the Winter Palace in St Petersburg; with the men in full uniform and the ladies in Russian national costume, it was the most picturesque wedding of all Queen Victoria's children. The bride quite mollified the Queen by her willingness to carry a bouquet of white Osborne myrtle and by having the Orthodox ceremony followed at once by a Church of England service conducted by the Dean of Westminster, with Alfred's brother Arthur as best man. A few days later a Te Deum was sung in the cathedral in Moscow at which the bride and groom and all the Imperial family were present. At last Affie was well and truly married. Vicky, who was present at all these ceremonies, reported to the Queen that 'Dear Affie looks so radiant and beaming and really another creature— his satisfaction makes him so amiable to everyone.'

Marie saw Windsor for the first time on a March day full of brilliant sunshine. The town was gay with flags and the cheers of the crowds were enough to warm the heart of a young and home-sick bride. That night at a banquet in St George's Hall the new duchess of Edinburgh did her country and her husband credit with her happy looks, her charm and her wonderful sapphires and emeralds. But the magnificence of her dowry did not mean half as much to Queen Victoria as the fact that this Russian princess was 'not a bit afraid of Affie and I hope will have the very best influence on him'.

5

Helena

'Nature certainly divides her gifts strangely'

PRINCESS HELENA, WHO was born on 25 May 1846, came into the world a 'blue baby' after the Queen had suffered a severe and protracted labour. Nevertheless, the child recovered more quickly than the mother and grew up to be physically the toughest of the royal sisters.

Her childhood was uncomplicated. She did not aggravate with tearing rages, obstinacy or a tendency to answer back, neither was she docile or easily crushed; in her own way she had the reply to brotherly bullying or teasing—a swift and accurately-aimed punch on the nose. She was not ambitious, nor was she troubled by a great desire for knowledge, yet she was not stupid and did what was required of her correctly and neatly if in a somewhat uninspired way. In fact everything about Helena (or 'Lenchen', the diminutive of affection) was straightforward and reasonable—there were no dark corners anywhere. Because she was even-tempered and jolly she got away with a great deal that was censured in Vicky and Alice, both of whom were emotional and therefore much more trouble. She was not at all artistic—drawing and painting did not interest her in the least—nor did she learn to embroider like her sisters: it was a family joke that Lenchen was all fingers and thumbs and could not be trusted to sew on a button. No one was surprised that she had a heavy hand with music too; anyone passing the music room while Lenchen was having her lesson would hear Mrs Anderson's patient voice repeating 'lighter, Princess Helena, lighter', as her pupil thumped out scales or a simple exercise. Nevertheless, everyone acknowledged that she was a persevering child who deserved praise for never giving up;

she always did her best and if that best was not good enough she was neither scolded nor told to do it again. On the other hand her copy-books were always neat and she was quick at arithmetic, and although her essays were more plodding than imaginative she made up for that by the absence of blots and erasures. She knew that Vicky and Alice were cleverer than she was and accepted the fact without rancour, never minding that she was overshadowed by their greater intelligence, since nobody made the comparison to her disadvantage. Queen Victoria enjoyed teaching her far more than she did the others; Lenchen's very ordinariness was a foil to Vicky's cleverness—the way her eldest daughter raced on ahead disconcerted her, while Alice had been too deep for comfort. The governesses recognised that Lenchen's lack of competitiveness in the schoolroom was a good influence on the others; she was not touchy, never set one against the other and could be relied on to be fair if it came to a quarrel.

Horses were her great passion. Nothing pleased her more than to be given a spirited animal to ride, especially if it had a history for being unmanageable. She could calm a frightened horse quickly and easily, with a sensitivity and understanding she never showed in the schoolroom. If she had been a modern princess she would have spent most of her spare time in jodhpurs or jeans exercising her horses, mucking out or practising for show-jumping competitions, for she had enormous powers of endurance. Opportunities like these would have enabled her to develop that competitive spirit so lacking in her lessons. As it was she had to conform to convention, trail about in long skirts (which she hated) and ride side-saddle, a style she found so restricting that she envied her brothers and longed to be a boy. Lessons with her father were a little delayed in Lenchen's case (Albert usually began them at fourteen), not because she had no academic bent but because in 1860 Albert was very much occupied with affairs of state and deep in a lengthy correspondence with Vicky in Berlin about European politics, so that to spend half the evening with Lenchen would have meant him going to bed even later and rising even earlier than usual. Besides, Victoria and Albert had come to the conclusion that it was better in every way to defer lessons with the younger ones in order to prolong their childhood and push marriage further away. The result was more freedom for Lenchen to ride for hours on end while her parents were busy with other things.

Balmoral was without doubt Lenchen's favourite home, and she never remembered a time when she was not happy there. Of course she rode at Windsor and Osborne too but she could not do so in the same abandoned way, nor go out in all weathers, returning home with a ravenous appetite and sleeping like a top. Because the opportunities were not so great at Osborne, she took to the sea as second best, getting a thrill from steering the *Fairy* through rough weather, for she could be trusted just as much as her brothers to do nothing foolish. Albert soon noticed that Lenchen understood the way machines worked far better than Bertie, who disliked getting covered in grease, and almost as well as the mechanically-minded Alfred. Her hair tied back with an old piece of ribbon (to her mother's despair she never cared how she looked), she would spend hours below decks learning exactly how steam worked. Every kind of physical activity appealed to her. She could swim better than Vicky and Alice although much younger, was always grumbling that running races against girls was no fun, scandalised the court by turning cartwheels and was often to be seen in bitter weather watching Eton football; yet although tough with a deep voice and long strides, Lenchen was not at all masculine but simply one of those girls nature intended for an athlete. Unhappily, the conventions of her age decreed that she must not develop those talents that came most easily to her.

Her father's death when she was only fifteen closed for ever Lenchen's chances of satisfying her frustrated energies, because it removed the one stimulus which could have turned them in other directions. On that awful December evening she stood at the foot of the bed white and trembling and watched the father she loved draw his last breath. The shock was terrible. Not once had it occurred to her that he could die while she was still more or less a child and while they all needed him. Quite naturally she had fallen into the Queen's habit of 'consulting Papa' on any question she could not solve herself, so that in her own way she too had come to regard him as 'an oracle'.

It had been her father who had allowed, even encouraged, her to spend so much time in the stables grooming her horses herself and generally looking after their welfare. More than once she had noticed him watching her taking them over jumps, a pair of binoculars in his hand, and her heart swelled with love at the thought that he had taken the trouble. It had been her father who understood how she was fascinated by machinery and everything mechanical (instead of making fun of her like the others) and did not scold her for making her hands rough and for not taking more interest in feminine matters. He never made her feel small for her dislike of cooking in the Swiss cottage, and had always understood her preference for make-believe battles in the boys' home-made fort or a turn in the carpenter's shop.

Without especially thinking about it she had looked forward to her coming out as a sign of emancipation and quite liked to picture herself dressed in white, roses in her hair, a fan in her hand, opening the ball with her father. She knew what it would be like, for on 10 February 1860 she had been allowed to attend the dance given at Buckingham Palace to celebrate her parents' twenty-first wedding anniversary. Not long before this Queen Victoria had been in despair about Lenchen's appearance; 'her features are again so very large and long that it spoils her looks', she told Vicky. In fact Lenchen possessed a 'strong' face, as her father realised and he predicted that when she 'grew into her looks' she would be handsome in a stately way, if not exactly pretty.

But soon all thoughts of this kind had to be put behind her, for with the bulwark of their lives removed everything came to a full stop; there was no coming-out ball, no riding in an open carriage to Ascot, no young princes for her to look over. Yet although perfectly happy at home, Lenchen was a normal girl and looked forward to marriage with the right person. Even her confirmation in April 1862 was in the Queen's words 'an awful day'. Instead of the happy celebration the others had enjoyed she was made to wear the simplest of white dresses and was catechised in Albert's room in the presence of her mother with reminders of their loss all about them. The air of mourning added poignancy to an occasion that was solemn at the best of times, and there was no present table, no large luncheon afterwards at which she would have been principal figure.

A dark curtain had come down on her life. Although in years to come Lenchen remembered her father a great deal better than did the last four children, the image of a cheerful affectionate human being round whom all the fun revolved, the man who would swing baby Beatrice in a table napkin or run races with them all on the sands was, alas, to fade and be replaced by the saintly prince of Queen Victoria's imagination.

Full of sympathy for Lenchen's deprivations, Vicky took her under her wing after Albert's death and invited her young sister to pay several visits to Prussia. Although the two girls discussed 'adored Papa' and found him faultless, Vicky's picture of her dead father was far truer than her mother's and she did everything in her power to imprint the proper image on Lenchen's mind—that he was not an angel so shocked by the misery of the world that he had to leave it, but a man who saw the wretchedness of life clearly and worked to alleviate it. It was during these visits that Vicky taught Lenchen to be patient with the grieving Queen and convinced her that her mother was not an hysterical woman but a wounded animal brought low through shock.

Thus a girl who possessed no remarkable qualities became a stablilising influence in a household where all was gloom and youth had to live in the shadow of death. No one dared be cheerful in the Queen's presence, no one dared show pleasure in the coming of spring and the long warm days of summer. For the Queen's young family to have to suffer the loss of a father they loved was bad enough, but to have to demonstrate this grief constantly, without relief of any kind was a terrible strain. Alice bore the marks of it for the rest of her life and so in various ways did the others, but Lenchen's commonsense was strong enough to bring a breath of refreshing normality into this atmosphere of mourning. Because she was not so tactless as her younger sister Louise she could get away with a great deal that the other could not. Queen Victoria trusted her, knew that she never embroidered a story or made mischief among her brothers and sisters—and in her widowhood the Queen was far too prone to accuse her children of mischief-making and going against the wishes of their 'mother and sovereign'. Alice who had once been her great support came in for more than her fair share of the Queen's wrath on this account. The best side of Queen Victoria longed for her children to be happy, especially in their marriages (and it was because she feared that Lenchen was becoming too fat to attract a husband that she nagged her about her hearty appetite), but when she remembered her own lonely state she could hardly bear to see their happiness.

In the autumn of 1862 Lenchen's lot was lightened by the arrival of Alexandra of Denmark for a month's inspection as Bertie's bride, an ordeal enough to daunt the spirits of the strongest-minded girl. But the sixteen-year-old Alexandra was natural, tender and kind and at once she and Lenchen became bosom friends, shared confidences like sisters and spent a lot of time giggling and laughing together. Queen Victoria noticed the intimacy and it was a mark of her esteem for Lenchen that it enhanced Alexandra in her eyes; it also made the Danish princess's visit a great deal easier.

Almost imperceptibly Lenchen became more of a prop to her mother than the Queen realised. During a pilgrimage to Coburg in September 1863 (she had by this time already settled into the pattern she was to follow for some years, that of a mourning recluse) she became alarmed by hearing that the Emperor of Austria was about to visit her there. She need not have worried; quite naturally and without fuss, Lenchen stepped into the breach and took the whole burden of the visit off her mother's shoulders. Without either of them realising it, the Queen clung pathetically to this practical daughter, whose 'no nonsense' attitude and quiet efficiency made life more bearable for her. She wrote to Vicky that 'Baby [Beatrice] perhaps as well as poor Lenchen are the only two who still love me the most of anything—for all the others have other objects . . .'.

How long could it be before Lenchen too had another 'object' to love and protect from the vicissitudes of life? Much to Queen Victoria's indignation there were rumours as early as 1861 that 'if Princess Alice would not have the Prince of Orange as a husband, he was willing to wait for Princess Helena'. In 1863 the danger of having Lenchen carried away to a foreign country came frighteningly close when Vicky tried to make a match between her sister and Prince Albrecht of Prussia (known as 'Abbat') who proposed coming to England to take a look at this marriageable princess. The Queen was told, and at once set her face against such a union. By now Lenchen was acknowledged as her mother's amanuensis, cheerful companion and protector from the outside world. The thought of her living hundreds of miles away like Vicky was unbearable, and although no doubt the next daughter would be pressed into taking over Lenchen's duties, Louise was less suited to the rôle because she was artistic, unpractical, lively and opinionated and much less easily appeased than her sister. The Queen did not picture Louise sitting down placidly and uncomplainingly to copy out letters for her mother. So she clung to Lenchen, half-hoping that marriage was not for her or could be postponed indefinitely. She was encouraged in this by Lenchen's homely appearance, which compared badly with the delicate loveliness of Louise. She only half-regretted Lenchen's plain face and poor figure when she wrote to Vicky, 'poor, dear Lenchen, though most useful and active and clever and amiable, does not improve in looks and has great difficulties with her figure and her want of calm quiet graceful manners. Nature certainly divides her gifts strangely.' Nobody was surprised that it was Louise who caught all eyes when dressed for a Drawing Room but the Queen forgot that no one looked more superb on a horse than Lenchen. Because she was an outdoor girl, her complexion was not as soft or as fine as it might have been, but she always looked fit and well—for she loved nothing better than striding out in all weathers accompanied by half a dozen dogs, and thought nothing of returning home drenched to the skin after a long gallop on her favourite horse Jacoby.

It was fortunate that she was troubled neither by violent passions nor great desires, otherwise she might have rebelled at the many tedious little jobs that fell to her lot because nobody else would do them. Lenchen was too intelligent not to understand very well that if she wanted to spread her wings there was only one way to do it and that was in marriage. How marriage might be achieved she had no idea, but she clung to the thought as though to a lifeline. In 1865 that hope began to crystallise after a visit to Coburg the year before. Urged on by Vicky and Fritz, Prince Christian of Schleswig-Holstein had paid a surprise visit (otherwise it would never have been allowed) to Queen Victoria while she was staying at the Rosenau with Lenchen and Beatrice. Christian, who belonged to the unfortunate Augustenburg clan whom Bismarck had ruined, was almost forty-two, a big, burly, kindly man without home or fortune. The Queen liked him on sight and found him very pleasant to talk to and afterwards confided to Vicky that she 'felt safe' with him, a great compliment and a mark of confidence that warmed Vicky's match-making heart. To her delight Vicky noticed too that Christian was attracted to Lenchen. He saw, what others did not, that here was a young woman whom the world thought had nothing deeper in her character than an agreeable manner and plenty of commonsense, but who was lonely and longing to be loved for herself and to have a home, husband and children of her own.

In September 1865 the Queen wrote a long letter to Vicky which made the latter (who had secretly played destiny to her sister) smile to herself:

Prince Alfred and Princess Helena by Winterhalter

The Princess Royal, Princess Alice, Princess Helena
and Princess Louise by Winterhalter

I must now tell you in the strictest confidence what I could not before as after so many disappointments and difficulties I could not speak till I was sure—but what I have to say will please you and what you very likely suspected—viz there is a prospect of Lenchen marrying Christian of Holstein.

Before September was out it was all settled. Christian had agreed to live in England, at Frogmore in Windsor Great Park, which was fortunately vacant and lay conveniently close to the castle. He made no objection to Lenchen continuing to help her mother by deputising for her at Drawing Rooms ('everybody says no Drawing Room without me gives so much satisfaction as the ones held by Lenchen') and in many of the other duties the Queen could not face.

Queen Victoria's satisfaction at the marriage (Christian too had promised to do his bit towards helping her) had been strengthened by the untimely intervention of Alice who was out of favour at the time; Christian was too old a husband for a girl of twenty, she said, to the Queen's indignation. Who was Alice to stand in the way of her sister's happiness? And Lenchen was supremely happy, perfectly content with her Christian who looked years younger as soon as Queen Victoria took him in hand, thinner on her diet and healthier for being pushed out into the fresh air every day and not allowed to coddle himself.

There is no doubt that Queen Victoria enjoyed managing this docile man, turning his mind to profitable interests that would keep him busy. She saw to it that he took English lessons, learned to make a speech and conduct himself in public as her son-in-law. Above all she was overjoyed that the newly married pair were really happy to live close at hand and in England, a country in her estimation that was second to none—'the greenest and pleasantest land on the whole earth'. Her feelings are well expressed in this letter to Vicky, the recipient of all her woes and joys, written when Lenchen and Christian were on honeymoon in Paris: 'Lenchen is fortunate indeed I think to be able to liv in this blessed and peaceful land safe from all wars and troubles. I miss her very much, for it is not only the help, but the power of telling her everything which is such a great comfort.'

6

Louise

'She is in some ways very clever—and certainly
she has great taste and great talent for art . . .
but she is very odd, dreadfully contradictory,
very indiscreet and from that making mischief
very frequently'

PRINCESS LOUISE WAS born on 18 March 1848 in the middle of
pandemonium of a kind unprecedented in Buckingham Palace.
The whole Continent was ablaze with revolution, and there was a
general flight to Britain—'the land of the free', as Queen Victoria
remarked with a meaning look. Nevertheless, she and Albert
generously opened their doors at once to a stream of foreign
royalty made homeless and destitute by the conflagration. Victoria
was kept so busy organising their accommodation, although it
seemed impossible there could be any room left (her own children
had been moved into the servants' quarters) that her labour was
well advanced before she took to her bed.

The new baby was only three weeks old when she had her first
taste of travelling by train (it was to be her favourite mode of
transport, just as it was her father's) when the duke of Wellington
ordered the whole family to the Isle of Wight to escape the
Chartist riots that threatened the throne; he could not feel in a
position to manoeuvre, he said, while Her Majesty was at the
palace. Within a month all was normal again and they returned in
time for a sixth christening in eight years, when the baby received
the names Louise Alberta Caroline. The choir of St George's
Chapel sang the hymn 'Gotha', which Albert had composed to
while away restless evenings at Osborne when half his mind was
occupied with affairs of state. With a first line that began 'In Life's
gay morn', 'Gotha' was as far removed from riots and rebellions as
he could make it.

Unlike some of the Queen's and Albert's other children (even their mother owned that Bertie and Leopold were 'quite frightful' at birth) Louise was undeniably pretty. Lady Augusta Bruce talks of her with feeling as 'that delicious baby Louise', and delicious to look at she remained even in old age. Her fair hair was light and fluffy but easily manageable, curling naturally round her small but shapely head, her large eyes were a spectacular shade of deep blue with long lashes, and she had a small nose and a chin which did not recede but stuck out determinedly when she wanted her own way. As a child she was nearly always lively and alert with occasional sudden bursts of moodiness which her favourite governess Madame Rollande likened to English summer weather, all sunshine one moment, dark as thunder the next. Her mother found her perplexing to a degree and was never quite sure whether, because she was born in strange times, Louise was very clever or just plain backward. In the long run, it was better to call it the artistic temperament, for clever Louise certainly proved herself to be, although perhaps she did not have as much depth to her intellect as Vicky or Alice. However, even without trying very hard, she managed to get on with her lessons well enough; her governesses were always quite satisfied with her while admitting that she showed no special aptitude for anything except drawing, at which she excelled. Apart from this, her greatest assets were the beauty and charm which developed from an inborn knowledge of how to use her good looks to the fullest extent. Without being either vain or selfish she knew very well that she was by far the prettiest of the sisters and did everything that she could to enhance her beauty. As she became a woman this took on the fashionable Pre-Raphaelite look but was saved from insipidity by the interest and amusement with which she gazed on the extraordinary world in which she had the good fortune to live. Beautiful, talented, and a princess, she knew that she was born to be cherished and that everything would fall into her lap as of right.

She was the only one of the girls to be called by Albert's dead mother's name. In her deep emotional needs, in the waywardness and the intelligence which she never quite turned to proper use, she resembled the grandmother who had died many years before she was born. As had been the case with the other Louise, part of her nature was to remain unsatisfied throughout her life.

Like all the others she learned to ride, skate, swim and dance as a matter of course and like them too she spoke German and French from infancy, but she was outstanding in none of these accomplishments. Yet when at the age of three Louise was given her first painting lessons by Edward Corbould it was seen at once that this was where her true vocation lay. From that moment a pencil and paint brush were hardly ever out of her hands, and she would be happy for hours drawing landscapes from memory or illustrating a book that had been read to her. For Louise, sketching took the place of the stories the others wrote for their own amusement. It was fortunate that Corbould never set her to make slavish copies of well-known pictures as most nineteenth-century young ladies were taught to do; instead he encouraged her to use her originality, especially if she was painting from nature.

The books used in the nursery and schoolroom had not changed much since Vicky's day: *Maynall's Questions* had not been replaced by anything more up to date. Louise waded through that and *Mauder's Treasury* without much enthusiasm, but she enjoyed reading exciting authors like Wilkie Collins (to whose books she was introduced by Vicky), and wept so copiously over Mrs Beecher Stowe's *Uncle Tom's Cabin* that it had to be taken from her, but she was never to be an avid reader like Vicky or Alice and did not arrange for books to be sent out to her from Mudie's library when her husband was Governor-General of Canada. She was not an outdoor girl like Lenchen either, although she loved to watch the Highland games and danced the sword dance with more verve and accuracy than any of her sisters. The artist in her took in the minutest details—she could remember the smallest differences in the cut of the uniforms of every regiment in the British Army, and compiled a sketch-book of these for her father's files. In 1873 she painted the Shah of Persia from memory after he had paid a short

State Visit to the Queen at Windsor. His appearance was a gift from heaven for a girl with an eye for colours like Louise, with his astrakhan cap, long gold-embroidered coat, the whole exotic get-up smothered in precious stones 'as though he had stepped out of the Arabian Nights'. Later on, drawing and painting were to become her greatest solace—sketching the rugged mountains and vast rivers of Canada, the wild animals that roamed freely in the hills, gave her a solid hold on life when she and her husband were drifting apart.

Albert died when Louise was thirteen years old. Although so young she was fetched from her bed to be a part of the gruesome death-bed scene. Frightened, incredulous and tearful, she stood holding tightly to her sister Lenchen's hand as they all filed slowly past to give farewell kisses to a father who already did not know them. Because of her youth the effect on her was transitory, and she would have recovered quite quickly had not a shutter come down on her life, blotting out all the delights that as a royal princess she had every right to expect; instead she had to stand by helpless and angry while the prospect of an exciting life of balls and receptions was snatched away from her and replaced by a monotonous routine of travelling between one home and another at set times of the year without any prospect of mixing with young people of her own age.

This bright sparkling star had to shine dimly in a mourning light. Even after Albert had been dead for four years and Louise was seventeen, Queen Victoria refused to open the Buckingham Palace ballroom for just one coming-out dance. Lenchen had accepted this prohibition philosophically. After all, what did a stuffy old ball matter? But Louise was devastated, and refused to reconcile herself to the loss; the effect of this lack of pleasure and fun on her spirits was lowering, to say the least, and almost overnight she began to suffer from 'nerves'. The ghillies' ball at Balmoral, a rough-and-ready affair at the best of times, was no substitute; besides, Louise hated (as they all did) to see her mother dancing reels with the uncouth John Brown, who was master of ceremonies on these occasions.

Fortunately Vicky had not forgotten the young sister whose frustrations she guessed were damaging her health. She knew enough of the set-up at home to read between the lines of complaining letters from her mother (especially during 1869) about Louise: 'she is in some ways very clever—and certainly she has great taste and great talent for art which dear Lenchen has not, but she is very odd, dreadfully contradictory, very indiscreet and from that making mischief very frequently'.

Vicky's answer was to invite Louise to Berlin. There she noticed the stir her sister's beauty caused among the Prussian princes in the crowded and overheated ballrooms of the royal palaces. With amusement she watched Louise making an entrance, floating gracefully into a room to become the instant cynosure of all eyes in a pale-coloured dress of the lightest material—for although not particularly interested in fashion, Louise knew instinctively what set off her beauty to perfection. It took courage for a royal princess to eschew the heavy dark cloth and jet beads which turned many young English girls into matrons as soon as they were out of the schoolroom. She also refused to crimp her hair with curling tongs, preferring to let it hang loosely round her shoulders or to pile it up softly on top of her head—both styles which made her look more ethereal than ever.

At first the Prussian princes, used to a very different kind of woman, were taken aback by this lovely young creature who chatted vivaciously and in the most natural way in the world with men and women alike. Puzzled though they were, they were attracted to her like moths to a flame as soon as they got more used to her 'strangeness', although her air of self-assurance and independence continued to disconcert them. Some of them were daring enough to approach Vicky with marriage intentions, but although she had cleverly hidden her repugnance Louise thoroughly disliked the uncouth Prussians whom she met in Potsdam and Berlin; their arrogance and heel-clicking and the atrocious way they treated women, all made her shudder. Besides, they had no sense of humour at all and did not laugh when she told them what she thought amusing—how, having been 'Lady Louise Kent' to the Queen's 'Countess of Kent' when they were travelling abroad incognito, she continued to use the title after their return in order to make fun of her mother. To be in the company of men who did not think this a joke set her teeth on edge and put her once and for all against marriage with a foreigner.

She was not sorry to be home again, but one good thing resulted from this holiday in Germany. The respite had given both the Queen and Louise time to think, and although matters were still far from perfect between them the weeks with Vicky had done something to make Louise see the Queen's unhappiness in a better light. She was not so quick to give offence with loud remarks like 'Mama was not too unwell to open Parliament, only unwilling' which hurt the Queen and made her look small. Improved though Louise was, she had not changed so much that she could tolerate any better the montonous to-ing and fro-ing that continued as regularly as the seasons between Windsor, Balmoral, and Osborne; the sense of utter boredom almost amounting to desolation that the Household so rightly called 'Balmorality' would seize her in the Highlands to such an extent that all good resolutions would fly out of the window and she would take a positive delight in mocking at everything, vexing her mother very much by her indiscretions. One autumn, when the Queen delayed returning from Scotland by making Louise's sprained knee the excuse to stay another fortnight, the incorrigible girl loudly proclaimed that if she had injured herself in London no concessions would have been made on her account, but she would have been bundled into the train willy-nilly. It was incidents like these that caused Queen Victoria to write peevishly to Vicky that Louise was 'very strange and difficult'.

With great good sense Vicky urged her mother to allow Louise to join a painting course at the National Art Training School (now the Royal College of Art) which Albert had founded out of the profits of the Great Exhibition. Times were changing, she said, and

Princess Helena by Winterhalter

Princess Louise, Prince Arthur and Prince Leopold
by Winterhalter

it would not make Louise any less bohemian in her habits to keep her unoccupied and disgruntled at home—besides, it was a pity to waste her talent for art. A further inducement to let Louise have her own way was the encouragement given her by the sculptress Mrs Thornycroft (at that time engaged on busts of the royal family), who with the Queen's consent introduced her to the Hungarian Elgar Boehm and persuaded him to give her lessons in sculpture.

Here at last was the beginning of freedom. Her discontent disappeared when she discovered that at the art school she could throw off the trappings of royalty and become a student pure and simple, judged by her abilities alone. At nineteen she made a further bid for freedom and asked to be allowed to live in a studio of her own, but this brave attempt at independence was not permitted. In her wildest moments Louise dreamed of becoming a professional sculptress, for she had fallen under the influence of Boehm and had become very skilled at catching a likeness, although her style was too sentimental and limited. She was much influenced by the Pre-Raphaelite painters, many of whom became her friends, but partly because of her position as a daughter of the Queen and partly because she could not entirely throw conventions to the winds, she never became really close to them. She turned her back on the Impressionists and the Rodin school of sculpture, and showed no more curiosity to go over to Paris and see their work for herself than did the Pre-Raphaelites. Somehow the originality that Edward Corbould had noticed when she was young did not quite materialise. Technically clever though her paintings are, they could have been done by any skilful amateur of her generation. Only in some almost casual sketches which aim at no special effect is there some spark of the talent that never quite came to fruition. Nevertheless, she rates high when judged by the standards of her time (as her lifesized sculpture of the Queen shows), and other artists showed their respect by electing her to the honorary fellowship of the Royal Society of Painters and Etchers.

By the time Louise was twenty, experience had taught her that as a member of the royal family it was useless to pretend that she was the same as everyone else. This had the effect of making her calmer and more resigned to her status, although it did not mean that she was willing to become her mother's amanuensis, to make trite speeches in public, open bazaars and be generally useful like Lenchen and Beatrice. Nevertheless, she became almost overnight easier to live with, and no longer did her mother see only the bad side of her difficult daughter. So quickly did the Queen learn to understand this child of hers that on Louise's twentieth birthday she wrote to Vicky a very different kind of letter from the complaining ones of old. 'She is (and who would some years ago have thought it?) a clever, dear girl with a fine strong character, unselfish and affectionate.' The impossible had happened. The Queen and Louise had drawn close, a warmth had sprung up between them that was to increase with the years and the effect on them both was excellent. With tact and patience Louise persuaded her mother to sing again, something she had not had the heart to do since Albert's death, with the result that invitations to give concerts at Buckingham Palace were once more sent to musicians of every degree, from the celebrated violinist Joachim down to a string of lesser men like the young Italian pianist Alfonso Renardo and a Welsh harpist, a Mr Ap Thomas, who had only just come to London, for like her father before her Louise sought out the talented but as yet unknown. All this did a great deal for the Queen who began to feel that she was becoming a patron of the arts as Albert would have wanted; it took her out of herself and gave her a new lease of life. For this Louise was entirely responsible.

This new closeness between mother and daughter came just in time for Queen Victoria to accept Louise's marriage to a subject, an alliance so unusual that the family strongly opposed it. For at twenty-two Louise had fallen in love with Lord Lorne, the eldest son of the duke of Argyll and a Liberal member of parliament. Needless to say, Queen Victoria triumphed, despite rude remarks from the Prussian King and Queen—she was quite well able to deal with those. 'I thought you would prefer this', she wrote to Vicky on 1 November 1870, 'to a small German prince who would have been the only alternative. A second Prussian marriage ... would have been very unpopular here and a poor, small German prince also.'

The whole country was behind the Queen in this new style royal marriage. The public was sick and tired of good English money being spent abroad and especially of having hordes of Germans coming to the English court with their large suites and ridiculous manners. Louise, too, had certainly had enough of German princes and wanted to continue to live in her own country. It was left to Queen Victoria, an old hand at putting people in their places, to tell Vicky that the marriage had called forth a great burst of delight; it was, she said, 'the most popular act of my reign'.

7

Arthur

'The best child I ever saw'

'ARTHUR IS A precious love, really the best child I ever saw', Queen Victoria wrote to Vicky in April 1859 as her third son and seventh child was approaching his eighth birthday. In his mother's eyes he always remained the 'best child', only rivalled in her affections by his youngest sister Beatrice.

The new baby (christened Arthur Patrick Albert) was born on 1 May 1850. It was soon clear that he was a strong, healthy baby; the nourishment provided by his Welsh wet nurse agreed with him, and when he was weaned he was not sick like Vicky nor a bad feeder like Alice. He did not turn a hair when vaccinated; it 'took' the first time, whereas most of the others had had to have the operation done all over again and convulsed the nursery with their screams. He cut his teeth without trouble, no horrid-tasting lotion had to be rubbed on his gums, nor was Mr Brown called upon to lance the skin. He walked at the proper age, his legs were the straightest of all the children and he had the pluck of his brother Alfred without his recklessness; he never cried when he fell and cut his knees and—wonder of wonders—he seemed to have none of that irritability and quick temper that made the childhood of the others such a trial. His calm unruffled nature, slow to anger and quick to forgive, never caused his parents the slightest anxiety or trouble.

The date of his birth caused a stir in the newspapers which made much of the fact that it was the duke of Wellington's eighty-first birthday, that he was named after the hero of Waterloo and that Wellington was his godfather. The boy must be a soldier too, the papers said. Whether he was indoctrinated from birth or whether it was coincidence, none can tell, but a soldier Arthur became. From the moment he could sit up and take notice he would always clap his hands at the sight of a red coat, while the sound of a military band made him shriek with delight. Whenever they were at Windsor his nurse had to take him to the terrace every day to see the sentries marching backwards and forwards, and it was unthinkable that he should miss the spectacle of the changing of the guard at Buckingham Palace. On his first birthday his pride and joy was a toy drum, and his lisped pronouncement to the Household that 'Arta is going to be a soldier' caused no surprise.

As he got older the placid baby grew into a shy boy with a diffident nature who, like his father at the same age, was miserable when he had to meet strangers. He would become very white, and his eyes would fill with tears when compelled to face them, but he would nevertheless march resolutely forward, shake hands or give a smart military salute. Without consciously thinking about it, his parents fostered this son's passion for soldiering. Something military was always placed in a prominent position on Arthur's present table: for Christmas 1855 he was given an exact replica of Guards uniform complete with bearskin and sword, as well as yet another box of lead soldiers to add to his collection of the regiments of the British army. After Vicky's marriage he began to collect the Prussian regiments too, and to amass information about their history. His father called him 'Colonel Mentioner' (presumably after some favourite phrase like 'I only want to mention . . .') and it became such a joke between them that when he wrote to Arthur he would always address him in this way. The fort that Albert built at Osborne with his elder son's help was used to better purpose by Arthur and from an early age he would play in it for hours on end, planning battles and manoeuvres with his large assortment of toy soldiers while he lay on his stomach behind one of the miniature cannon standing at the four corners of the fort. All too often his big brothers wanted to take charge of these games and there would be battles of another sort in which Arthur came out badly, so that his favourite companion was a father who was only too happy to reconstruct for his son's benefit the manoeuvres he had seen his uncle Leopold direct on the plains outside Brussels. King Leopold soon became Arthur's hero, because he had fought in the Prussian army against the great Napoleon, and the boy never tired of hearing his father tell exciting tales of his exploits.

It was always a wrench for Arthur to leave Osborne, his precious fort and the imaginary companions with whom he peopled it when his father was occupied elsewhere, for this child was very inclined to be a 'loner', though not an unhappy one. In the Highlands he had to be more gregarious, but even on family expeditions the peaks and crags fired his imagination with quite a different kind of warfare, the primitive bloodthirsty struggles between the Picts and Scots. In the long Balmoral evenings he would read all about these tribes, their feuds and their fierce conflicts. It was quite usual to find him alone working out a skirmish as true to the customs of those days as he could make it. His head was so filled with the fascinating lives of imaginary human beings that he was much quieter than the other children. He never had to be slapped down for talking out of turn, never begged for 'treats' or clamoured for his parents' attention, with the result that Queen Victoria was inclined to indulge him more than the others. Once, when quite young, he was allowed to stay up until midnight for a ghillies' dance. As the clock struck he was still on the floor taking part in a reel, feet flying, kilt swirling, and his fond Mama noticed with satisfaction that, small though he was, he would not allow himself to be left out. More than the others he loved the children's dances held at Buckingham Palace, and we read of him at the age of five opening the ball with his mother, looking (she said) 'so pretty' with a dirk stuck in his sock to show off his 'long, straight legs'. These legs of Arthur's were a source of some pride to Queen Victoria who thought she could tell by their legs whether her sons would grow up to be tall like their father (she had a weakness for tall men) or short and squat like the men on the 'wrong side' of the Coburg family. In a long letter to Vicky, written after a particularly satisfactory children's ball, she could not help contrasting

Arthur's 'good legs' with those of the sons of Prince Augustus of Saxe-Coburg-Kohary (who came from the 'wrong side'). 'Poor Philippe's legs', she wrote, 'looked as though they were stuffed.'

Although it was evident early on that Arthur was not clever like his two eldest sisters, yet he possessed in full measure what Victoria and Albert looked on as a sign of great character: industry and perseverance. Bertie, for instance, was neither industrious nor clever nor painstaking, nor was he interested in anything. Much would have been forgiven him if he had been just one of these. Arthur, the Queen told herself, would never become an unco-operative adolescent, lounging about, hands in pockets, doing nothing at all. Arthur never knew what it was to be bored. If he was not playing with his soldiers, he would be found sorting and labelling his collection of Wellington relics, or deep in an account of the Peninsular War. Before the age of fifteen he had become quite an expert on Wellington and Napoleon.

Although not at all interested in sketching scenery, he had a passion for drawing maps, especially those showing famous battles, and he took infinite pains to get these correct. Albert enjoyed drawing maps too, and because of their mutual interests the Queen always talked of Arthur as 'so like dearest Papa'; in fact, except for a few mannerisms which he could have picked up when young, Arthur resembled his father in very little and had nothing of Albert's powerful intellect. If Albert had not died so young, Arthur's education would have been better and he might have made more of his talents, but he was deprived of his father's guiding hand at the time when he needed it most. From the age of eleven he had to accustom himself to a totally new way of life. He accepted the gloom that came with his mother's widowhood philosophically and with remarkable understanding, and while it drove his brother Alfred away it kept Arthur by his mother's side. Unlike Affie, Arthur did not blame the Queen for her tears and irritability, her dislike of noise, her recoil from everything that smacked of enjoyment, but showed towards her a tenderness and sensitivity far in advance of his years.

Because he had never expected to die so soon, Albert had made no special arrangements for the education of the younger children. Only one thing had been settled about Arthur—on reaching the right age he should be allowed to enter the army if he still wished it. Albert did not mean by this that Arthur should not have as rigorous an education as the others, for he had a 'perfect horror' of uneducated officers and had done everything in his power to raise the standard of education in the army and was still doing so at the time of his death. Arthur was only eleven in 1861, but ready for more serious work, yet Victoria was too prostrated with grief to give much thought to his schooling, so his education was somewhat haphazard instead of intelligently planned. Major Elphinstone, his tutor, was a charming and kindly man but no intellectual, and there was no Mr Birch or Mr Gibbs (either would have suited Arthur very well) to awaken the boy's interest in the things of the mind.

His creative side was never properly awakened, nor did anyone help him to cultivate an appreciation of art in any form. In Arthur's extensive travels there is no mention of a visit to Florence or Rome to see pictures or architecture, not a word that a piece of sculpture thrilled him by its beauty. He never collected paintings, books or beautiful furniture, as his father did, nor had he much time for music.

Like his sister Alice before him, Arthur was a late developer and one of the reasons may have been that he was never brought on by a wider education at the right age. Vicky, with her broad range of interests, might have done something to help her brother if she had not been so far away and so absorbed in her own young family and her own problems. However she did advise her mother to allow Arthur to see something of the world, and was very scathing about the way German princes were tied to their parents' apron strings and never given independence. In 1863 a start was made in this direction when Major Elphinstone took the thirteen-year-old boy on a walking-tour of North Wales. No one knew who he was and Major Elphinstone was delighted at the natural way Arthur talked to people, his eagerness to be polite overcoming his shyness, and at the agility with which he climbed Cader Idris, never grumbling or complaining that he was tired. The next year they undertook a more ambitious walking-tour in Switzerland, following the route his father and Ernest had taken when they were students at Bonn. In the spring of 1865, Arthur spent his fifteenth birthday on board the *Enchantress* travelling in the near East, and followed this by a tour of Turkey. The next year he was allowed to join Bertie on a tour of Greece. So it went on: Arthur was hardly ever at home in his formative years, and like his brother Alfred he missed a great deal of the closeness of family life. He was pushed out of the nest early and a soldier's life kept him out for many years more. In all this time there was no one to help him conquer his diffidence or give him the affection he needed. In consequence the 'happy loner' became something of a withdrawn solitary, with the result that he suffered from a feeling of inferiority all his life.

When he stayed with Vicky he felt too ignorant to open his mouth in front of his clever sister or voice an opinion on anything of importance (although his views were in fact often well thought out and sensible) and too afraid of showing his lack of knowledge in conversation with her circle of intellectual friends. Therefore he did not enjoy himself in Prussia as much as he might have done. Once he became a soldier he could not repair past neglect by his own efforts, for he soon discovered that there was no time for self-education. It was a pity that the habit of reading or visiting exhibitions had never been formed in youth.

Nevertheless, there were many signs that Arthur was intelligent and sensitive. He saw very clearly that his mother thought him nearly as flawless as she had thought his father, and that any fall from grace might have serious consequences for her. It was a serious burden for a young man to bear, and he tried hard to avoid any protracted stay at Windsor or Balmoral, where he was forced to behave in an abnormally circumspect manner. He kept a constant guard on his tongue, never contradicting the Queen like Bertie or Affie and never rebelling at restraint like Leopold. The

Court did not complain that he was rude nor the servants that he was inconsiderate; guests found him sweet-tempered and helpful and admired the way he was constantly attentive to the Queen. In as mixed a household as any in the land this needed a special kind of humour and a high degree of self-discipline. How often he turned the other cheek we shall never know.

A letter the Queen wrote to Vicky after Arthur's confirmation in 1866 shows how unreasonably high a standard she set for him. 'Dear boy, he is so innocent, so amiable and affectionate that I tremble to think to what his pure heart and mind may be exposed. There is no blemish, no fault like there was in poor Affie—no falsehoods and want of principle, nothing but real goodness. Oh may God keep him so . . .' There were certainly no 'falsehoods or want of principle' in him (and here the Queen is very unfair to Alfred) but did she think that Arthur had learned nothing on those travels of his? Two years later Queen Victoria is still writing in the same vein, again most unwisely comparing him with Affie to the latter's disadvantage. After enumerating her second son's many faults she writes: 'But there is a bright spot in another direction on which I love to dwell and that is Arthur. . . .' Not even Vicky pointed out to her mother that she was laying up trouble for herself by turning Arthur into a saint on earth as she had turned Albert into a saint in Heaven and that to do so was most unfair and wrong.

In July 1866 Arthur was sent to Woolwich to begin his soldier's training. Life among officer cadets at that time was pretty raffish; there was always a war going on somewhere in the world and the risk of sudden death was ever present, so a soldier wanted to get everything he could out of life while he was alive and in one piece. Queen Victoria did her best to protect Arthur's virtue by insisting that he live at the Ranger's House in Greenwich Park. In every other way, she said, she wished him to be treated like an ordinary officer. But she was quite certain of one thing: Arthur's 'purity' would protect him from sin.

Arthur enjoyed being a soldier. It was the life he had been preparing himself for since he was born, and he could therefore be cheerful about its hardships. Moreover, his enjoyment was plain for others to see, so that when in 1868 he did a spell of duty in Ireland (as much a trouble-spot then as now), his agreeable manners and good nature made an excellent impression. Queen Victoria was jubilant and wrote extravagantly to Vicky that Arthur had had 'a perfect triumph in Ireland, even in the worst and most dangerous parts'.

Whenever it was possible Queen Victoria loved to have this handsome son by her side, especially on state occasions when he could be relied on to do the right thing; he never looked sulky, made gaffes or tried to slink away early, and because he had travelled so widely he always had something interesting to say to foreign potentates. The Queen knew that Arthur would go to any lengths not to hurt anyone's feelings and rather naughtily played on this and on the fact that to do the right thing at the right moment was second nature to him. An instance of this was at a palace banquet in 1877 when he did not forget to toast his mother as Queen and Empress of India in accordance with the new title she had just assumed, something Bertie had conspicuously failed to do at a similar function the week before. 'Arthur is just like dearest Papa', the Queen wrote to Vicky, describing what happened. Never once did it occur to her that she was in danger of turning Arthur into a mother's boy and that he only avoided it by keeping his life in separate compartments, one of them as far away from his mother as possible. But he seems to have understood more than the others the weight of the burden ('unlike that of any other Mother in the world', as the Queen was fond of saying) that had fallen on to the Queen's shoulders since Albert's death and that there were times when she felt at her wits' end with affairs of state and the peccadilloes of her numerous brood. On at least three occasions Arthur was present when an attempt was made on his mother's life, and saw the courage she displayed. She was always at her best on the most testing occasions, for though she may have been selfish in her widowhood, she was never petty. Arthur understood this and never hurt her feelings by showing that he wished for independence. If ever he did show some trifling sign of individualism it was sure to be remarked on by a Mama who disliked change in any shape or form. When, after a spell in Canada where high collars were all the rage, he dared wear in her presence what she called 'those monstrous stickups', she scolded him soundly for imitating his fashion-conscious brother in this and by cutting his hair. It took two tactful letters from Vicky to make her see sense: 'The collars you object to so much have grown much smaller and I do not think he wears his hair in an unbecoming fashion, though it is cut rather short.'

In 1872 Vicky had a chance to measure a maturer Arthur against young Prussian officers when he spent a holiday with her and Fritz in the Neue Palais in Potsdam. She found him very much more cultivated than they were, despite the gaps in his education, besides which his shyness was a protection from the attentions of Fritz's licentious relations, who made no attempt to lure him away for a 'bit of sport'. He was easy to entertain and asked nothing more than to go shooting with Fritz or to wander with Vicky round the little farm at Bornstädt admiring the improvements. It was on this visit that Arthur first saw Louise, the youngest of the three daughters of Prince Frederick Karl of Prussia (known as the Red Prince), a cruel father and husband who was estranged from his wife Marianne, one of Vicky's closest friends. But Louise was still a child so Arthur had to wait two years before he saw her again.

This Prussian princess was not pretty or striking in any way and she too was painfully shy; but something about her, perhaps a longing to be protected, appealed to Arthur and he fell deeply in love. The Queen thought that her handsome Arthur was throwing himself away on a plain girl, and half-hoped that he might fall for some ravishing Grand Duchess when he acted as best man at his brother Affie's wedding in St Petersburg. When he remained faithful to Louise she confided in Vicky that she could not understand why Arthur needed to get married at all! However, with her usual good sense she gave in and later generously conceded that her beloved Arthur could not have chosen better.

8

Leopold

'Child of anxiety'

QUEEN VICTORIA CALLED her fourth son her 'child of anxiety', and so he remained for every day of the thirty-one years of his short life.

At first it seemed as though everything to do with Leopold's arrival in the world went better for his mother than ever before. His birth on 7 April 1853 became a pleasant experience because for the first time the Queen was given chloroform administered (a drop or two on a handkerchief rolled into a funnel) by the well-known anaesthetist Dr John Snow of Edinburgh under the watchful eye of Sir James Clark who attended Queen Victoria in all her confinements. Since this was an easy birth the Queen recovered rapidly, was cheerful and good-tempered and never suffered at all from sleeplessness, depression or irritability. Her one regret was that the other children had not been born with the help of this wonderful new pain-killer, for which she had proved to be such an excellent subject.

Unfortunately, Leopold George Duncan Albert did not thrive as well as the others born under greater strain and stress. He was thin, his cry was feeble and he was frequently sick. Sir James Clark mistakenly put all this down to a weak digestion and merely suggested a change of wet nurse, with milk less rich. For a time the child seemed to improve and to fill out a little, so Sir James Clark was congratulated on his perspicacity. Later, when he began to walk, frequently falling down as children do, it was noticed that he bruised easily and cried out as though in pain. Soon it was discovered that 'little Leo' was suffering from the rare and in those days untreatable disease haemophilia, a condition transmitted by a female to a male in which bleeding cannot be stopped. From this moment on his parents' peace of mind was gone for ever. Queen Victoria in particular tried to protect this delicate boy from accidents of any kind by over-anxious care which Leopold expended precious energy in resisting, for his great ambition was to be treated like everyone else. His father's attitude was more matter of fact; there were no haemophiliacs in his family and he took the line that Leopold would outgrow it, as he would the epilepsy which attacked him before he was a year old.

Very delicate Leopold may have been, but he made up for ill health by an unquenchable spirit and an intellect which promised to be as good as that of his eldest sister. He learned to read easily as invalid children often do, but after that his nose was never out of a book and his choice of reading was often remarkably advanced. Like Vicky, too, when she was young, he would amuse himself by slyly confounding his elders with awkward questions to which he already knew the answers. He was barely five when he wanted to know all about the paintings which hung on the walls of his father's study at Osborne; for some reason Duccio's 'Virgin and Child' fascinated him. Before long he was becoming quite know-ledgeable about early Italian art. On the days when he had to lie on his sofa to recover from some minor accident that might have major consequences, Albert's inventiveness came as a godsend; the boy was allowed as a great privilege to use his father's paint-box and at first Albert guided the small frail hand, showing him how to make patterns that in turn could become a picture, a discovery that delighted the child. When the sofa became too unbearable for the patience of a boy whose instincts were far from those of an invalid, Albert would carry him about in his arms so that Leopold could see what the others were doing, but it made him sad to notice how this featherweight longed to join in the rough-and-tumbles of childhood games. On good days Mrs Anderson gave him piano lessons, and it soon became apparent that music was his passion and that his progress was astonishingly rapid. He loved to sing too, and it was strange to hear a strong voice coming out of

Queen Victoria with the infant Prince Arthur
by Winterhalter

Prince Arthur by Winterhalter

such a fragile body. Albert often sang duets with him to the great
satisfaction of both, but it was a pity that he could not spend nearly
as much time with Leopold as he would have wished, since he
knew better than anyone how to handle the child. Even when
Leopold was confined to bed Albert refused to show that he was
sorry for him and always behaved as if there were nothing unusual
in his being segregated from the other children. It was the only
way to quieten his fears and help him keep a hold on life.

Queen Victoria always described Leopold as ugly. When he
was five she wrote to Vicky that 'he holds himself still as badly
as ever and is very ugly'; in fairness she added that 'he is a very
clever, amusing but absurd child'. When he started to grow she
was in despair, telling Vicky that 'he holds himself worse than
ever and is a very common-looking child'. She longed to improve
his deportment, but nothing she did had any effect because of his
terrible disease: 'he has still a most strange face, sadly out of drawing, and holds himself too awfully'. It was not in the Queen's
nature to flatter her children (she criticised even a pretty girl like
Louise in case her beauty might encourage vanity), but these
criticisms of Leopold must be taken with a pinch of salt. In fact,
although not good-looking like Arthur, Leopold had an interesting face with a lively expression and huge eyes that seemed to
burn in his head and to look out defiantly on a world in which
he was debarred from doing everything that he most enjoyed.

The great difficulty in dealing with Leopold arose from his wilful nature; he was as strong-minded as his mother and would not
do as he was told. His illness had been explained to him, and the
need for care, and he was too intelligent not to understand perfectly well. So long as Albert lived there were compensations for
lying on a sofa all day because his father would always find time
for him and never thought him a nuisance. Albert never fussed
him, was always interested in his doings and (most important)
made Leopold feel that he was part of the busy life that went on
round him. Moreover, Albert was helping him to overcome the
slight speech defect which was a consequence of his epilepsy;

because it made him conspicuous for the wrong reasons, Leopold hated it and was sensitive about it.

Between bouts of illness he was allowed to ride, take part in amateur theatricals, and go for country walks to hunt for geological specimens for the collection he was making in imitation of the one begun by his father and uncle when they were the same age. Then Leopold would be as happy as the day was long, his mind filled with all sorts of projects. Trouble always began when the family moved to Balmoral, however. The crisp air so invigorated the child that he could not be restrained; of course accidents happened, and poor Leopold would find himself once more in bed, a doctor in constant attendance. At Osborne in May 1861 he caught measles from Alice's fiancé Louis of Hesse and nearly died. It was unfortunate that for once his father was much too busy with his own work, as well as the Queen's (she had had a nervous breakdown following her mother's death in March), to be much with the child. In poor health himself (he was to die seven months later) Albert wanted to fulfil an engagement with the Horticultural Society and went off to London, taking the reluctant Queen with him. It was uncharacteristic behaviour on his part to leave Leopold without both parents when so ill, but the most likely explanation is that he thought the Queen's obvious concern was making the boy anxious about himself and thus weakening his already frail constitution. They were speedily recalled to find Leopold at death's door. But his indomitable will to live prevailed and he recovered, although slowly. It was decided to send him to convalesce in the mild climate of the South of France in the autumn under the care of Sir Edward Bowater, a veteran of Waterloo. But ill health dogged them both. All seemed to be going well when Sir Edward was taken ill and by 30 November 1861 the Queen and Albert heard that he was sinking. Before a satisfactory replacement could be found Albert himself was dead.

The shock of his father's death affected Leopold badly; he became unruly and defiant and suffered one accident after another with their awful consequences—the dreaded internal bleeding.

The Queen was desperate with worry. She loved him dearly and each attack terrified her more, especially now that there was no husband to reassure her that all would be well. Leopold knew that his time was short, but he wanted to make the most of what life he had. The sad and solitary existence he was forced to lead sickened him, and as soon as he was old enough to do so he defied scoldings and slipped the leading reins at every opportunity.

At fifteen, Leopold again hovered on the brink of death. On holiday at Osborne he had been playing vigorous games with his brother Bertie's children when he fell with the usual results, an attack of internal bleeding. He was very ill indeed, but as soon as he was able to sit up he demanded to be allowed to continue his Latin and Greek lessons with his tutor Mr Duckworth. Already he was fluent in French, German and Italian and was keenly interested in politics. He would lie in bed, propped up by pillows, devouring the newspapers, excitedly discussing everything that interested him with anyone who cared to listen. The Queen marvelled that Albert's brains could flourish in so frail a body. The moment he was out of danger he begged to be allowed to have his two young nephews with him, and the Queen noticed that strong and healthy though they were, the boys had not half the mental vigour of their young uncle. Leopold loved children and was devoted to his pretty sister-in-law Alix, who was the only one who could influence him in one of his stubborn moods. His devotion dated from the day in November 1862 when Alexandra came to Osborne for a month, before her marriage to Bertie. As the only male member of the family at hand, Leopold was sent to the landing stage to meet her, a bouquet of flowers in his arms. Shy and awkward, he wondered how he should explain who he was and at what point he should present her with the flowers, but immediately she landed all difficulties dissolved as Alexandra rushed forward and kissed him.

That he had to be denied so much pleasure in life, that he was not free to go to balls, dinners, shoots or out in society generally, so worried Vicky that she pointed out to the Queen that once

Leopold came of age she would not be able to restrain him. What would happen then? Might not his fine disposition become soured? Surely it was better to let him have some fun now, she pleaded, than none at all? 'A young man pining for liberty is not likely to make the best use of it once he gets it within his reach!'

Of course Leopold knew very well that everything the Queen did was intended for his good, and he was really devoted to her. Nevertheless, he rated his own independence highly and longed to be like other men. Queen Victoria argued her own case from the heart: 'Since '62 I have never been any distance from Leopold', and again 'no one knows the constant fear I am in about him'. Yet Leopold was only human, and he chafed at being treated all the time like an invalid. Short sharp quarrels were not uncommon between then, since Leopold was not in the least afraid to answer back.

> *Queen to Leopold:* 'I heard your musical-box playing most clearly this afternoon, even as far off as your room.'
> *Leopold:* 'Impossible, for my musical box never plays.'
> *Queen:* 'But I know it was your musical-box—there was that drum in it I recognised.'
> *Leopold:* 'That shows it wasn't my musical-box, there is no drum in it.'

But the Queen needed Leopold's support often enough. She recognised that he had an old head on young shoulders and often came out with some perceptive remark that would help her make up her mind on some perplexing point; and his advice, when she asked for it, was sensible. He helped her on state occasions too, for he was an easy conversationalist and not at all self-conscious, so that because of her shyness she was only too glad to have him by her side. Yet she dare not let him overtire himself, dreaded all exertion for him and was happiest (as she thought he was too) when she had him quietly to herself with only his young sister Beatrice for company, playing duets with her or accompanying her and Beatrice when they sang. She tried to deceive herself that he was happiest with peaceful occupations like this—until suddenly he would be off like a streak of lightning she knew not where.

When Leopold announced without warning that he was going up to Oxford, the Queen opposed the plan vigorously—he would not be happy at that 'odious place', he was not strong enough, she needed him at home—but he did not give a fig for her objections. Like his father before him he was supremely happy with quiet ordinary things like attending lectures and writing essays, and still more with the companionship of men of letters like Ruskin, with whom he became immediately friendly. The sound of bells soothed his restless spirit and he forgot for a while that his life hung by a thread, for his was a nature from which hope sprang eternal.

It was at Oxford that for the first and only time he tasted the joy of leading a normal life. He went to concerts and heard some of the finest musicians of the day, among them the violinist Peisiger, a pupil of Joachim's, who had lived in Berlin and had played to Vicky's accompaniment. Learning, too, drew him like a magnet, for there was so much he wanted to know and so little time for it. At the annual dinner of a scientific society he experienced the supreme pleasure of making a speech in which he had the opportunity to refer many times to the father who was still very much alive to him.

He was at Oxford in 1873 (and enjoying better health than usual) when he was shaken out of his fool's paradise by the death of his six-year-old nephew and godson 'Frittie', who was also a haemophiliac. Perhaps the letter Leopold wrote to his sister Alice, the boy's mother, after this tragedy shows the depth of his own physical and mental suffering:

I cannot help saying to myself that it is perhaps better that this dear child has been spared all the trials and possible miseries of a life of ill health like mine, for instance. Oh dear Alice, I know what it is to suffer as he would have suffered and the great trial of not being able to enjoy life or to know what happiness is like others. That old saying 'everything works for good' seems always to me such a truly comforting and good one. When first darling Frittie was taken away from among us, I remember so well people saying 'it is all for the best', he would never have been well, etc., and I said to myself 'if anything happens to me that is what everybody will say' and it made me feel so bitter for a time but I think I have come round to see the justness of the saying which I quoted. . . .

1878 was year of crisis and resolution for Leopold. He was now twenty-six and ready, even longing, to live his own life whatever the consequences. His mind made up, he confronted his mother, told her that he was sick and tired of the boredom of Balmoral, and flatly refused to accompany her on her next visit north. This was open rebellion (almost as bad, to her, as renouncing his faith) and at first the Queen could not believe her ears. Never for one moment had she imagined that the home Albert had created for her, where they had spent so many idyllic holidays together, could be repugnant to anyone, let alone a child of his. Queen Victoria had become so blind to the feelings of other people that she had no idea that not only her children but her entire household loathed the enforced seclusion of Balmoral, which was no longer the gay happy home of Albert's time (when even such a severe critic of royalty as Greville the diarist had to admit that a holiday in this highland home was soothing to the nerves). The household word for the frustration and boredom was 'Balmorality'. It was a reaction against 'Balmorality' which made Leopold determined to spend his holiday somewhere else among congenial people of his own age. On the rare occasions when there had been some fun like dancing or amateur theatricals, Leopold was banished to his room in case the excitement proved too much for him. He bitterly resented this affront to his manhood. Now that he was taking the law into his own hands and going where life was pleasant, the Queen was bewildered and furious—but fury was uppermost. 'Leopold must not think he has carried the day and put me down', she wrote angrily to Vicky after this act of defiance.

She suspected that he had gone to Bertie and Alix to racket around with 'that fast set' and kill himself into the bargain. Deviously she tried to make Vicky persuade him not to stay at Marlborough House but at Buckingham Palace (if he must stay in London), 'where he cannot so easily get in and out'. Of course Leopold saw through this little ploy and straight away went off to Paris for two weeks. 'It is too abominable', the Queen wrote to Vicky, seething with indignation. Part of her anger was caused by the fact that she missed his witty conversation and the way he always managed to help her enjoy life twice as much as anyone else, and she longed to have him back. In the end discretion won the day. She would try persuasion and an appeal to his 'better feelings'.

Although she held no brief for dukes ('for I always say no one can be a prince, but anyone can be a duke') Queen Victoria had created Leopold Duke of Albany in 1881 and had given him the Garter two years earlier than his brothers in case he did not live to receive it. Leopold understood the reason very well and would have given up both dukedom and Garter for a single year of perfect health.

Living normally meant marriage to Leopold as much as it did to the others, but this was something the Queen dreaded. Not only did she not want to lose his advice and support but she was afraid he might receive a rebuff, for she could not imagine that any sensible girl would want to take him on. In fact the ideal girl fell in love with him; Princess Helen of Waldeck-Pyrmont, who was not in the least timid but as outspoken as Queen Victoria herself. Moreover, she was charming, well-read and clever, and also quite prepared to help the Queen since there was nothing at all stiff and German about her. They were married on 27 April 1882 and ten months later there was another grand-daughter to add to the already formidable number. With a daughter-in-law to share the 'awful anxiety' about Leopold's health, Queen Victoria was able to relax and not become agitated when he took more exercise than was good for him. No longer did she fret and fume when after a strenuous game of golf Leopold was laid up for three weeks with a painful knee, a huge price to pay for a few hours' pleasure. He had made his choice—as far as he was able he would live like other people.

The spring of 1884 was particularly cold, with biting east winds and frost at night. In order to escape the worst of the bad weather Leopold consented to go for a week or two to Cannes, although his wife was expecting a second baby. While there he injured the knee of his already enfeebled leg and within twenty-four hours he was dead. He was thirty-one years old and had been married for only two years.

Queen Victoria was anguished by his death. Wilful and defiant though this son of hers had been, the cause of many a sleepless night, he was also very dear to her heart; she spoke the truth when she said his intellect was very like his father's. Albert's sensitivity, his compassion, his longing to be of use to the world, his thirst for knowledge, all lived on in this tall thin delicate young man; even Albert's love of beauty had not passed him by.

It was cruel that proper employment was denied him because of ill-health so that he was made to feel inadequate. Sir Henry Ponsonby, the Queen's Private Secretary, once heard him say vehemently that if he was not given something useful to do soon he would take matters into his own hands and stand for Parliament. 'In what interest?' asked his equerry. 'Extreme radical,' came the reply. That this was said at Balmoral after a game of billiards with John Bright may have had something to do with it, but had not his father been accused of socialism? Albert's reply to the charge had been just as swift—if caring for those who could not care for themselves was socialism, he was all for it.

9

Beatrice

'The only one who needs me now'

'SHE WELL DESERVES being loved, for a dearer, sweeter, more amiable and unselfish child I never found, and she is the comfort and blessing of my declining years, "Benjamina" as Aunt Alexandrine calls her.' Queen Victoria wrote this to Vicky when Beatrice was fourteen years old. It was well-earned praise, for according to Queen Victoria not only was Beatrice all these things, but she was the only one of her children without that streak of touchiness which made the others so difficult to deal with in certain moods. In every way 'Baby', as she was called for far too long, was a most uncomplicated child—born, so her mother believed, for one purpose only: to keep her from losing her reason when she was left a widow in December 1861. 'I live only for Beatrice', she would say mournfully, 'the only one who needs me now.' The truth of course was just the opposite; it was the Queen who needed Beatrice and needed her so much that she was determined to keep her by her side unmarried for the rest of her life.

No greater misfortune could have happened to this ninth and last child of Victoria and Albert (born on 14 April 1857 when her parents had been married seventeen years and Vicky was already engaged) than to lose her father when she was only four. From that moment the Queen's reliance on her deepened, until everyone took it for granted that there was no question that 'Benjamina' would remain at home to be her grieving mother's right hand and chief comforter. What Beatrice's state would be after her mother's death (a lonely unwanted spinster perhaps?) the Queen never bothered to consider, nor the sacrifice she was demanding; it was enough that Beatrice never seemed to wish for a separate existence like the others but was content with her lot.

So long as Albert lived, Beatrice occupied a privileged position. All rules were relaxed for the youngest, who was allowed to stay up late, come down nightly for dessert, join in the others' treats and say what she liked without let or hindrance, for her parents had come to realise that it made very little difference to a child's eventual development whether these things were permitted or not. Of course the result was that she was somewhat spoilt by doting parents and brothers and sisters who played with her as though she was some kind of remarkable talking doll, but she was saved from the bad effects of over-attention by her charm, her winning personality and her beauty. 'Quite the prettiest of us all, she is like a little fairy,' was Vicky's opinion of this large healthy child who was to become a decidedly sturdy young woman.

At her christening (when she was given the names Beatrice Mary Victoria Feodora) Vicky and Fritz of Prussia were of an age to be her chief sponsors, and at two she was already an aunt. Then the consequences of being the youngest of a large family were suddenly changed. By the time she was four she was being indoctrinated into believing that she must 'never leave Mama', a rule of life that she accepted without question; there is not a single letter that hints at resentment or rebellion of even the mildest kind, so that everyone came to believe that this was what Beatrice herself wanted.

Although Albert died when she was so young, Beatrice always insisted to the end of her life (she lived until 1944) that she could remember her father perfectly, and had a clear picture of herself sitting on his knee while he played the piano, being taught to sing nursery rhymes, running to his dressing room in the morning to watch him shave and being allowed to feed the little bird that lived in a cage in his room and that could say 'Guten Morgen'. Other glimpses of childhood remained with her too: Papa reading to her, teaching her to draw, strapping her on to Tommy, her first pony.

Then suddenly the blinds were drawn, her mother put on black clothes and her 'sad cap', and laughter and happiness were forbidden. The effect on a young child born as Beatrice had been to noise and freedom, to sing and shout and run from room to room as she pleased, was traumatic. Death was a condition that she could not understand but she knew it meant tears, darkness and change. The Queen made no attempt to shield Beatrice from the agony of her own grief; on the contrary she clung with all the tenacity of her nature to this baby for the comfort and security no one else could give her now. With Albert gone, Beatrice became doubly precious; she was his last-born, his plaything, his pet, and her very existence had a special significance that her mother was determined to remember. She was the only one of Albert's children in Windsor Castle the night he died who was not brought to the death chamber to watch her father's life ebb away. The story goes that when all was over and the stunned Queen had been undressed, she suddenly ran barefoot to Beatrice's room, lifted her out of her cot without waking her, wrapped her in one of Albert's nightshirts and carried the sleeping child to her own bed. If the story is true, this sudden impulse to draw comfort from Beatrice was a most symbolic gesture.

Although she was equable and not easily cast down, nevertheless the little girl was sensitive; she learned quickly never to ask when Papa was coming home. Yet it was only very slowly that she came to understand that she would never see him again. Why he had left them all was an enigma nobody thought it necessary to explain to her and the unanswered question remained like a lump in her throat, until the truth gradually dawned as she grew older. Even Vicky, when she came to England, in the spring, spent longer trying to give the Queen the will to live again (a task she performed with a breaking heart) than in explaining the cruel facts of life to her baby sister, whom, like everyone else, she thought too young to understand.

Only one person saw that something must be said to Beatrice, if only very briefly, and that was her nurse Thurston ('Turton') who had taken over from Mrs Sly in 1845. That spring and summer, when the Queen was incarcerated at Osborne, this sensible woman insisted on taking the child away from the house of mourning for a whole day at a time so that for a short spell she could behave normally—laugh, shout, run about, be a child again. Admirable as this was, it could have no long-term effect, and almost imperceptibly Beatrice's nature began to change. The lively, amusing little girl became quieter and less obstreperous; she learned to move softly, to shut doors without making a sound, to laugh less and less. She had always been quick at repartee and her funny sayings acted on the Queen like a kind of therapy in the early days of her widowhood (it never failed to bring a smile to her mother's lips to be asked 'Is it the salt I eat with my chicken?' when she told the story of Lot's wife), but after a time these too dried up and the spontaneity and the artlessness of childhood were replaced by an awkward shyness that she had never shown before.

In order that Beatrice should not be deprived because she was fatherless, the Queen took great pains to plan her daughter's education according to what she imagined Albert would have wished. She wanted it to be a thorough one, and spent many an anxious hour working it out on paper. There had been changes in the schoolroom since Vicky's day. Lady Lyttelton had retired in 1855 (a loss that was looked on by one and all as a blow as great as a bereavement) and her place taken by Lady Catharine Barrington. Madame Rollande (Rollet) too had gone and so had Fräulein Grüner and Mlle Charrier. Now the post of the two last governesses was filled by one woman, the practical and sensible Fräulein Bauer, as plain-spoken as her looks, with only Mlle Norèle to perfect Beatrice's French. Fräulein Bauer was smaller even than the Queen, very vivacious, active and versatile, able to turn her hand to anything. Most important of all, she got on famously with her royal mistress, who quickly recognised her superior character and complete loyalty. Bauer was a rock in a schoolroom deprived of Albert's influence, and Queen Victoria felt she could safely leave everything in her hands. Miss Hildyard had been forced to retire in 1864 through ill-health, so that of the old troop only Mrs Anderson remained, and she was getting older. Her ability to teach children to play the piano was considerable, but after discovering that Beatrice could read music effortlessly (Leopold too had this gift) she advised the Queen to ask Sir Charles Hallé if he could give Beatrice more advanced lessons and suggested that the Italian singer Tosti should train her mezzo-soprano voice.

On the surface, Beatrice's educational régime looked severe, since every moment of the day seemed to be accounted for and only an hour or two in the afternoon left to accompany her mother on her drives. But the reality was far otherwise, for the Queen was continually taking her daughter away from her lessons to read to her, copy a letter for her, go sketching with her or take a walk whenever she was in urgent need of 'a mouthful of fresh air', in fact any excuse to have the child with her. Of course there were groans in the schoolroom, but what could they do? Fräulein Bauer went as far as she dared, but the Queen's wishes were law and the governesses salved their consciences by echoing Queen Victoria's words 'the child is such a good child' and did not want to be hard on her. The governesses' protests would have been stronger if Beatrice had been very clever like Vicky, but since she was not they took the line that the Queen must come first. Besides, they knew that Beatrice was deprived enough already. Because Albert was no longer alive, 'treats'—such a feature in the youthful lives of the other children—were cut out altogether. There were no 'marine excursions' (once the despair of Lady Lyttelton), no picnics in the hills above Balmoral, no pony explorations, no noisy bathing parties at Osborne or competitive digging on the sands (Leopold was forbidden to dig), no *tableaux vivants* like that in which Beatrice had made her stage debut when only a babe in arms, and Astley's tumblers came no more to perform in the courtyard at Windsor.

Unlike the others, Beatrice was deprived of playmates too and was forced to be continually in the company of adults. This made her old for her age in some respects and over-young in others, for even after she had entered her twenties her mother and the Household still treated her like a child. Because he was four years older and resented not being allowed to forget that he was delicate, Leopold refused to play with his sister and in consequence Beatrice had to make up her own games with only dolls for company. This may have done much for her imagination but it also helped to make her secretive and shy. Queen Victoria persisted in calling her 'Baby' until she was grown up, not realising that her reactions to life were anything but childlike. '"Baby" is always sweet tempered, good and obedient', ran one of the Queen's letters to Vicky—that is to say, she always fell in with her mother's plans without a murmur. It is disturbing to discover that Beatrice was almost always like this, and only occasionally acted like the child she still was. There were no tantrums, no sulks, no acts of defiance; her life consisted of a series of negatives with no highlights anywhere. No one could tell if she noticed the suffocating atmosphere which would have been so dangerously enervating to most people, yet somehow this strange girl managed never to allow the cosseting and protection to weaken her character.

As early as 1863, when she was only five, Beatrice was made to understand how the Queen detested even the very thought of marriage for those who served her. Her anger when Lady Augusta Bruce fell in love at the age of forty with Canon Stanley (later Dean of Westminster) was quite alarming to a child who was very attached to her mother's Lady-in-Waiting. She was puzzled to understand why the Queen thought this particular marriage 'unnecessary', since there had been several marriages in her own family (Beatrice had been a bridesmaid twice) and had often heard the Queen speculate on partners for her brothers and sisters. It set a train of thought going in her head—marriage was not for her. The Queen did nothing to contradict it, rather the reverse, for it soon became apparent to everyone that the awful word 'marriage' must never be mentioned in Beatrice's presence. She became so aware of this, so self-conscious about it that, as a teenage girl whose

only contact with men was a delicate brother, she would go cold
all over and shiver with apprehension if a man as much as sent a
flirtatious glance in her direction. Unlike Leopold (who was continually trying to slip through the net) Beatrice merely accepted
her over-protection both from men and from life in general.
Strong and healthy, she had little outlet for her vitality except
riding Tommy her pony and playing in the Swiss cottage, and
even this became less fun because there were no sisters to
share the domesticity with her. So she had a great deal of surplus
energy and no way to use it up, since all forms of entertainment
outside the palace were taboo. It was the Queen's wish that
Beatrice should be 'kept back' as much as possible . . . 'she will
be kept very quiet and at home which will be much better and
happier for her and for me', she told Vicky in a complacent letter
which did not convince her eldest daughter as much as she hoped.
Vicky understood that to be 'kept quiet and at home' meant that
Beatrice would not be in the slightest danger of being 'snapped
up'. No foreign princes were invited to Buckingham Palace and
no young English noblemen were allowed within yards of her,
so that the Queen felt very safe indeed, especially since Beatrice
herself evinced no desire to be up and off into a home of her own.
She had seen enough of the battles with Leopold to wish to pit
her will against her mother's.

At sixteen 'Baby' was much taller than her mother, but even
so the Queen postponed her confirmation as long as she dared:
'I keep her as young and childlike as I can'. This act of faith had
been with the other girls the occasion to turn them overnight into
marriageable women. Not so with Beatrice. In her letter to Vicky
describing the event (which took place in January 1874), the Queen
made it clear that in this case there was to be no such change. 'I
never saw anyone look more simple, pure, innocent and sweet
than this dear good child did. She looked so very young—and her
very plain white silk dress—beautiful complexion and very fine
fair hair which she wears quite simply and plainly (and wishes to
continue to do) was very suitable.'

Although the Queen saw little difference between her baby at seventeen and the engaging child of three, members of the Household noticed how shy and retiring Beatrice had become, always standing close to her mother and eating her meals almost in silence. Good dinner-table conversation was a thing that had died with Albert and what talk there was the Queen kept in her own hands, so that invitations to dine were not sought after. Nor by this time was Beatrice sought after. Even at her mother's table she sensed that she was criticised and shrank into herself. Now that she had been confirmed, Beatrice should have been encouraged to spread her wings a little, perhaps be sent to Vicky in Potsdam for a few weeks or to Alice in Darmstadt, even on a cruise with Bertie and Alix. No doubt Queen Victoria would have allowed one of these but for her incessant fear that her only unmarried daughter, her prop and stay, might fall in love, perhaps with some foreign prince who would carry her off to his own country. It may have been merely to convince herself, but Queen Victoria repeatedly said that Beatrice was happy at home and wanted to remain there. Everyone about her had heard the Queen say that marriage was a lottery but that she herself had been particularly fortunate, yet this had not prevented her being on pins to get her other daughters married off with all speed. It was one of the many contradictions in her character. When challenged by Vicky, the Queen had replied that 'youngest daughters have a duty to widowed mothers' and she urged Vicky to keep her last child, Margaret, with her when Fritz died in 1888. But Vicky replied that 'Mossy deserved her happiness as much as the others'.

Nevertheless, as the years went by there were rumours of wedding bells for Beatrice; her name was frequently linked with the Prince Imperial, the Prince of Orange, several Prussian princes and even the eldest son of a wealthy landowner. The Queen's vehement support for the Bill to legalise marriage with a deceased wife's sister put about the report that she wished her youngest daughter to marry her dead sister Alice's husband Louis of Hesse, who had six children to look after. But nothing came of the Bill, nor of the Queen's plans (if there were any, which does not seem likely). Beatrice had been a bridesmaid several times already, now it looked as though she might have to face the humiliation of walking behind one of her own nieces, Charlotte of Prussia, who had every intention of marrying young. Was Beatrice to be always a bridesmaid and never a bride?

Although 'kept back' in many ways, Beatrice was not shielded from the stresses and strains of the day, for she had been born into troubled times. Her birth in April 1857 practically coincided with the Indian Mutiny, she was weaned to her parents' anguished moans after the terrible massacres at Cawnpore, and her first steps alone went almost unremarked because of the attempted assassination by Orsini of the Emperor and Empress of the French, an act which affected Victoria and Albert deeply because Orsini was domiciled in Britain. She was barely two when a cloud was cast over her home as soon as Vicky's terrified letters at Fritz's first venture into war in 1860 began to arrive by every post. At three she lost her father and at six she saw her family acrimoniously divided over Schleswig-Holstein, and she was only eight when the husbands of her two eldest sisters were fighting on opposite sides —civil war of a kind Queen Victoria said she never expected to live to see. By 1870 Bismarck had become a name to be dreaded, destroying the Queen's peace of mind and making her very anxious for Vicky and Fritz. Beatrice accepted the duty of keeping her mother optimistic all through the Franco-Prussian war, which was fought out in the drawing room at Windsor as well as on the battlefields of Lorraine.

Little went on in the government that Beatrice was not allowed to know since, unlike Bertie, she could be trusted. She understood exactly what the Queen thought of each minister, but she kept the knowledge to herself. Miraculously their opinions always coincided, so that when the family tried to prise Queen Victoria out of her seclusion, Beatrice refused to support them and sided with her mother. Now she too did not wish to be seen in public, and indeed was so little known that she could have gone shopping in Bond Street without being recognised. When the Queen consented to open the new St Thomas's Hospital, the public were amazed how tall and stately Beatrice had become but how childishly she was dressed. They were beginning to ask whether there was anyone about the Queen who could tell her that her daughter was grown up, since Beatrice had lost the ability to do so for herself. Unfortunately no one at Court had the courage and all her sisters were preoccupied with their own families.

Apart from a journey to Coburg at the age of seven to watch her mother unveil a statue of Albert, Beatrice's first trip abroad was to Lucerne which the Queen suddenly decided to visit in 1875. Beatrice enjoyed the experience so much that Victoria took her to Cimiez the following year and in 1879 as far as Italy in the hope that a warm climate would lessen the rheumatic pains in Beatrice's hands. An incident in Mentone in 1880, however, shows that travel abroad brought no escape from the virtual imprisonment which she suffered. She was invited aboard H.M.S. *Inflexible*, which was visiting the Riviera ports, but was so consumed with shyness at being in the company of men and without her mother for an hour or two, that she became tongue-tied and could barely speak above a whisper. Her nephews and nieces were beginning to look on her as a confirmed spinster, a sweet old maiden aunt although she was only twenty-three. They made joking remarks about her marriage prospects and when she went abroad alone for the first time to Aix-les-Bains in 1883 to take the cure for her increasing rheumatic pains, eyebrows were raised and there was speculation among the younger members of the family.

In April 1884 the Queen and Beatrice travelled to Darmstadt for the marriage of Alice's daughter Victoria of Hesse to Louis, the eldest of the three Battenburg brothers. Unknown to the Queen, the bridegroom had fancied Beatrice when he was in London a year or two earlier. He had dared to look at her with the mildest of flirtatious twinkles in his eye but Beatrice had felt in duty bound to snub him. Now he had found himself another bride. It was not altogether a happy occasion. Leopold had died in March and the Queen and Beatrice were only out of mourning for the wedding day itself; yet it was here in dim little Darmstadt where her sister had led such a narrow frustrated life that Beatrice at last found love—and under the very eyes of her mother too. Henry of Battenberg, the bridegroom's youngest brother, made advances to Beatrice and was not repulsed. Behind this love-affair lay the hand of Vicky who cunningly arranged that the two should be alone together while the Queen was too preoccupied elsewhere to notice what was happening. In fact her attention was focused for several days on securing an annulment of the recent marriage of her dead daughter Alice's husband to his mistress, while more momentous events were moving to a climax.

During the next two months Beatrice learned to her cost that the course of true love never runs smooth. When she plucked up courage to tell her mother that she wished to get married, the Queen was stunned. It was not Henry's status that bothered her (he was only a minor princeling and the child of a morganatic marriage) but the idea that she was, after all, to be left alone that was so appalling, and for a time there was a terrible rift between mother and daughter, who communicated by letter though still living under the same roof. Although thoroughly miserable, the Queen hardened her heart and refused to notice Beatrice's imploring looks. It was an estrangement that Henry himself mended by his charm, tact and gentle persuasion. Since Bismarck had reduced him and his family to penury after the war of 1866 as he had Lenchen's husband Christian of Holstein before him, there were no obstacles to his living in England and he convinced the Queen that she was gaining a son without losing her last and irreplaceable daughter.

The Children of Queen Victoria and Prince Albert

1. VICTORIA ADELAIDE MARY LOUISE, Princess Royal
Born 21 November 1840. Died 5 August 1901.
Married Prince Frederick William of Prussia, 25 January 1858 (he reigned as Emperor Frederick III of Germany from 9 March to 15 June 1888). Three sons, four daughters.

2. ALBERT EDWARD, Prince of Wales
Born 9 November 1841. Died 6 May 1910.
Married Princess Alexandra of Schleswig-Holstein-Sondeburg-Glücksburg, daughter of King Christian IX of Denmark, 10 March 1863. Succeeded as King Edward VII, 22 January 1901. Three sons, three daughters.

3. ALICE MAUD MARY
Born 25 April 1843. Died 14 December 1878.
Married Prince Frederick William Louis of Hesse-Darmstadt, 1 July 1862 (he succeeded as Grand Duke of Hesse-Darmstadt, 13 June 1877). Two sons, five daughters.

4. ALFRED ERNEST ALBERT
Born 6 August 1844. Died 30 July 1900.
Entered Royal Navy, August 1858. Chosen by Greek nation to succeed as King of Greece, but refused. Created Duke of Edinburgh and Earl of Ulster, 24 May 1866. In January 1867 as officer commanding H.M.S. *Galatea* embarked on voyage round the world (first English prince to visit Australia; shot at in Sydney), returning to England, 26 June 1868. Married Grand Duchess Marie Alexandrovna of Russia, 23 January 1874. Succeeded his uncle Ernest as Duke of Saxe-Coburg and Gotha, 22 August 1893. Four daughters, one son.

5. HELENA AUGUSTA VICTORIA
Born 25 May 1846. Died 9 June 1923.
Married Prince Christian of Schleswig-Holstein, 5 July 1866. Three sons, two daughters.

6. LOUISE CAROLINE ALBERTA
Born 18 March 1848. Died 3 December 1939.
Married John Campbell, Duke of Argyll, 21 March 1871. No children.

7. ARTHUR WILLIAM PATRICK ALBERT
Born 1 May 1850. Died 16 January 1942. Entered the Army, June 1868. Lt.-Col. commanding 1st Battalion, The Rifle Brigade, 1876. Created Duke of Connaught and Strathearn and Earl of Sussex, 24 May 1874. Married Louisa Margaret, daughter of Prince Friedrich Karl of Prussia, 13 March 1879. Governor-General of Canada, 1911–16. One son, two daughters.

8. LEOPOLD GEORGE DUNCAN ALBERT
Born 7 April 1853. Died 28 March 1884. Created Duke of Albany and Earl of Clarence, 24 May 1881. Married Helen Frederica Augusta of Waldeck-Pyrmont, 27 April 1882. One daughter, one son.

9. BEATRICE MAY VICTORIA FEODORE
Born 14 April 1857. Died 26 October 1944.
Married Henry, Prince of Battenberg, 23 July 1885. Two sons, one daughter.

Index